The Unofficial WITHDRAWN
Middle-earth
Monster's Guide

Hunt Hobbits, Hoard Treasure,
and Embrace Your Villainous Nature

The Mordor Collective

For more resources for writers, visit www.writersdigest.com.

To receive a free weekly e-mail newsletter delivering tips and up-
dates about writing and about Writer's Digest products, register directly at http://newsletters.fwpublications.com.

17 16 15 14 13 5 4 3 2 1

Distributed in Canada by Fraser Direct
100 Armstrong Avenue
Georgetown, Ontario, Canada L7G 5S4
Tel: (905) 877-4411

Distributed in the U.K. and Europe by F&W Media International
Brunel House, Newton Abbot, Devon, TQ12 4PU, England
Tel: (+44) 1626-323200, Fax: (+44) 1626-323319
E-mail: postmaster@davidandcharles.co.uk

Distributed in Australia by Capricorn Link
P.O. Box 704, Windsor, NSW 2756 Australia
Tel: (02) 4577-3555

Edited by Rachel Randall
Cover designed by Claudean Wheeler
Interior designed by Rachael Ward
Illustrations by Ben Patrick
Production coordinated by Debbie Thomas

media

Dedication

Peter: For Meredith O'Hayre. I couldn't ask for a better boss.

Scott: For Heather and for Harper.

Acknowledgments

Peter: Thanks very much to Scott Francis, my comrade in arms for this project. Thanks as well to our intrepid (and remarkably patient) editor, Rachel Randall.

Scott: Thanks to my co-author, Peter Archer; to my very patient and understanding editor, Rachel Randall, who probably should have destroyed all of us (but didn't); to Ben Patrick, who always draws cool things; to Claudean Wheeler for art directing when she'd rather design; and to my wife, Heather, for putting up with my crazy schedule.

About the Authors

Peter Archer is an editor at Adams Media in Avon, Massachusetts. Ever since reading Tolkien as a child, he's had a sneaking sympathy with the Dark Lord and welcomes this opportunity to indulge in his evil side. He lives in a converted two-hundred-year-old parsonage with his wife and two cats, who, if not precisely the embodiment of evil, at least personify the sins of Gluttony, Greed, and Sloth.

Scott Francis is a writer and an editor. His mom wanted him to study biology. "You were always so good at science," she used to say. But he is a writer and an editor. Visit him at www.seescottwrite.wordpress.com

Table of Contents

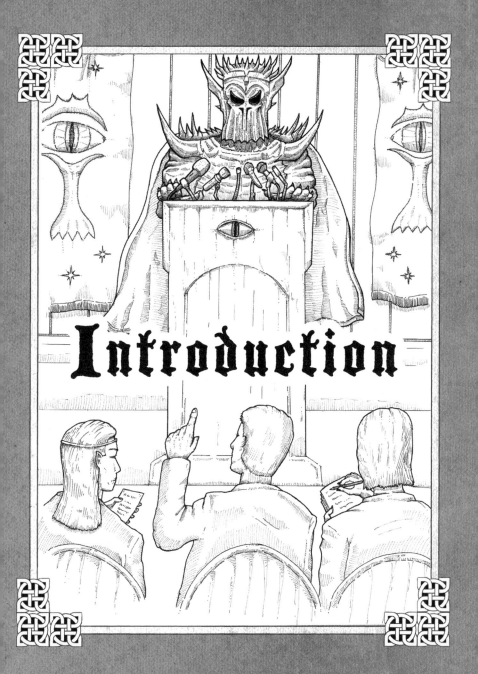

Introduction

Where to begin ...?

It was all Morgoth's fault. That's the place to start. I'm not saying our side didn't make some bad decisions—the One Ring may have been one of them, as I think back on it now—but mainly it was Morgoth's doing.

And the funny thing is, none of us ever thought Morgoth would've been so big on world domination. I had a couple of completely different candidates in mind. But that's the way it goes, isn't it? It's always the ones who seem completely in line with the program who suddenly turn around and start saying the Creators had it all wrong and they could do a better job.

As for me, well, all I really wanted was a bit of order. That's something that Middle-earth has always been lacking, and all I can say is that it's getting worse. In the Beginning, it was just the Elves who were always annoying, but now we've got Dwarves, Men (and women, apparently), ents, and goodness knows what else wandering around, sticking their noses into things that shouldn't concern them.

And halflings. Don't even get me started on halflings.

I can't even imagine where they came from. In my circles, we tend to keep a pretty close eye on who's going where in Middle-earth, but I certainly don't remember some little race of rat folk crossing the Baranduin and grabbing a piece of land for themselves. Of course, they claim they simply "settled" it, but we know what that really means: Kick out anyone (or anything) living there, grab as much land as you can, and hold onto it with both fists.

Typical thinking in the West. No attempt to establish a reasonable legal claim, no environmental impact studies, no cost-benefit analysis, no preinvasion geographic survey to see if the land can support a community. No interest in developing some powerful state apparatus like an army. In fact, as far as I can tell from the garbled reports I get from my scouts, the halflings don't even have an army. Can you imagine? A fat lot of luck the forces of Darkness would have had taking and keeping Mordor without an army. To say nothing of kicking Men out of Osgiliath (which wasn't even theirs in the first place!).

The first thing you do when you "settle" a place is establish a strong military perimeter. Then you police the interior to ensure the strictest possible order and control unexpected outbreaks of rebellion. After that you can turn your attention to things like food supplies for your troops, exploitation of natural resources, and so on.

Instead, these halflings have been fumbling along for millennia, while they ignore the outside world ... except insofar as they grow and export narcotics. Barrels of what they call "pipe-weed" have been found making their way as far East as Isengard. And if the halflings think for a minute that the forces of law and order in Middle-earth are going to sit still and let them turn its populace into drooling, weed-smoking, useless loafs ... well, they've got another thing coming.

The drug lords of the Shire are typical of the disorder that plagues this land. Let's look at another example: the Dwarves. Now, I'm not saying for a minute that the Dwarves haven't represented a problem in the past. But for a long time they were just a bunch of random wandering bands, content to pick up the odd payment for mining coal or jewels. It wasn't hard to keep track of them and make sure they didn't get into trouble.

But now look what's happened. First, there was that group that managed to make it all the way to Erebor and attack the dragon— along the way, they were responsible for the destruction of Laketown, but did they think to offer compensation for that? Of course not! In a rational society, multitudes of claims would have run through the courts for decades. But instead, they have to go and resolve the whole thing informally among themselves, just in time to form a military alliance and use it to attack an army of Orcs and Wargs that happened to be quietly passing through the area.

And now there are rumors that another pack of the ale-swilling idiots is on its way to Moria to "reclaim the ancient Dwarf halls." Hah! So much for faulty intelligence. If the Kraken doesn't get them, the Balrog will. It should take one good fortnight for them to be wiped out, if they don't perish on the journey first. Typical of the Dwarves to plunge into a situation they know nothing about, trusting to luck and the cosmic protection of that prize idiot Durin.

The attack on Erebor illustrates another point about the disorder and randomness that plague the lands. The dragon had taken the mountain from the Dwarves and held it by right of conquest. That's an old, established right. He was a perfectly reasonable beast, not overly expansionary in his aims, content with just a single mountain and his hoard. My point is that by every legal right—*every legal right*—that mountain belonged to him. The Dwarves lost. They left the area and should have stayed away permanently. They probably could have found another mountain and delved a city under it, if that's what they were so bound and determined to do. But no, they had to come moseying back to Erebor, trekking through Mirkwood as if they were on a picnic, and then show up at the dragon's front door, all muscle-bound and threatening. And after a series of very unpleasant encounters (unpleasant for the dragon, who lost a precious cup in the bargain), they provoked him into an attack on Laketown (*miles* away from where they were), where the poor thing managed to get himself killed. If there were any justice at all, those Dwarves would be dragged before a tribunal and forced to pay significant compensation to the dragon's heirs (if he had any).

This is so typical of the forces of Good—they can't see any viewpoint but their own. They can't manage for ten minutes at a time to be consistent. And at the first sight of something new and different, their instinct is to put an arrow in it.

"What about the Elves?" you say. "Surely the Elves aren't causing any problems."

You have no idea.

We don't deny that the Elves have an attachment to Middle-earth; however, Morgoth was there first and by primacy has the better claim. It is therefore completely reasonable and in line with Natural Law to assume that those who held allegiance to Morgoth should have prior claim over the Elves as far as the running of Middle-earth is concerned. That's perfectly reasonable, isn't it? Of course it is. The precedents I could show you ...

The second point is that for all of their "love" of Middle-earth, what are the Elves doing now? That's right! They're *leaving*. Going away. Abandoning ship.

I guess we can see now who really loves this place. You don't see the forces of Darkness going anywhere. No, we're content to stay and work with what we've got, making the best of a bad situation. But that's typical of the Elves and their "if it's not perfect, just abandon it" attitude. If you don't get it right the first time, don't try to fix it. Just walk away and start something else.

They were always a flighty, fidgety people. Short attention spans, all of them. No wonder they had a hard time getting anything done. I mean, think about it. What single monument to Elvishness exists? At least, comparable to, say, the Dark Tower, which you can see thirty miles off. Or even Mordor itself, which is a living tribute to the power of the forces of law and order. The Elves have had thousands of years, and what have they come up with?

Lembas.

It's enough to make one weep.

This is another thing. It's possible, when all is said and done, that if we lose this war through the interference of some little snot of a halfling being in the wrong place at the right time, the winners will write the history. And they'll say Mordor was evil, the Ring was evil, the Elves were the keepers of Good and Mercy and Justice ... blah, blah, blah. And then they'll turn around and go right back to their smug little lives, doing the same things they've always done, with the same rituals and same beliefs. Middle-earth will stagnate into a pleasant backwater. What we in the forces of Darkness really stand for is *progress*.

We want to see the world move ahead, to see it live up to its full potential. We want to see all that *mithril* that's under the earth pulled up and turned into something beautiful and useful. We want more efficient ways to grind grain, to raise crops, and to make weapons in order to spread enlightenment to other lands.

What's wrong with that? Isn't it better than doing nothing? That's what the Other Side is proposing—if they're not, like the Elves, just walking away from the whole mess.

The truth is, our side can't even be left in peace and quiet when it wants to. Take Dol Guldur. We retreated up there at the beginning of the age. It was quiet, out of the way, a nice sort of mountaintop retreat. Lots of lovely, cool breezes in the evenings; you could sit out on the battlements and watch the sun go down behind the Misty Mountains. We had pet spiders in the woods, and pet snakes and toads so tame they'd crawl up on your shoulder and eat food out of your hand.

And what's the first thing that happens? Some meddling idiot of a wizard comes wandering around, asking questions, poking through things, bothering everyone. Naturally, he was thrown out, but when has that ever stopped a wizard? They're the worst sort of interfering busybodies. Never content to leave things alone, never happy until they're controlling the world.

And they talk about the Dark Forces wanting a dictatorship. Hah! Just wait until the wizards are running things and see how you like it.

To be fair, they want law and order, too. It's just that the law and order they want is one in which they *are* the law, and they do the ordering.

Speaking of that sort of thing, let's talk about Men for a bit.

Men were a bit of a late addition to Middle-earth, and I can't say that they've worked out all that well. It was bad enough when we had the Númenoreans, but in typical human fashion they managed to blow themselves up. A few got out in time—enough to continue causing trouble.

I must say that of all the anarchic races that inhabit Middle-earth, Men are probably the worst. If there are two paths to a goal, one of them easy, efficient, and quick, and the other long, difficult, and resulting in the deaths of countless thousands, depend on Men to take the second alternative. It's almost remarkable to watch their consistency in this regard.

Mind you, some of them showed potential. Ar-Pharazôn, for example. There was a lad. No compunction about human sacrifice, no problem with making sure the laws were enforced. And he had an expansive, progressive mind as well. He was almost too good to be true. Ar-Pharazôn got an armada together to conquer Aman—and probably would have, since he had superb military planners, if I say so myself.

And then what happens? Just when things were going well, the Higher Powers step in and ruin everything. Drown the armada, knock over Númenor (well, it wasn't *my* doing!), and generally take us right back to square one.

Fortunately, although we now have more Men, at least they don't live as long. Five-hundred-year-old Númenoreans were getting to be a pain. But these days the worst of them don't seem to make it much past three hundred or so. That's something we'll have to keep working on.

The real problem with Men is that there are so many of them. The Elves are leaving Middle-earth, which solves that problem. The Dwarves don't reproduce in large numbers—and if you've ever seen a Dwarf female, you can understand why. Whatever numbers the halflings produce, at least they tend to stay in their own country. But Men keep making more of themselves and sprawling all over the place. Much faster than we can kill them off, although goodness knows we've been trying.

Just a few words here about magic rings, and about magic in general. To me, it's always seemed that magic is a bit of a cheat. When you want to conquer a domain, of course you can come in with all sorts of spells and magically conjured armies and resurrected dead, but it's easier and cleaner in the end to do the job with good old-fashioned elbow grease and a bunch of Orcs. As messy as it gets, there's actually a lot less to clean up afterwards than if you were using magic. For instance, some spells inevitably don't go off, and then a party of Orcs has to wander around the battlefield looking for Unexploded Spells (UXS). While Orcs are generally pretty obedient, I've known some to balk at that duty. I suppose you can't blame them. Who wants to bump into a spell that turns you inside out and wrings the blood from your veins? That certainly doesn't sound very comfortable. And then you've got to worry about magical residue, which can do some pretty nasty things to Orcs or anybody else who happens upon it.

Rings are another matter. Back in the day, they were very popular. For a while it seemed as if everyone in Middle-earth was clamoring for a magic ring. "Give me a magic ring so I can turn my Uncle Eoras into a toad." "I need a magic ring to make a girl fall in love with me." "I want endless riches, so make me a magic ring." You'd hardly believe some of the other things they wanted magic rings for. It's enough to make one blush.

In the end, the decision to make a limited edition of rings (twenty in all) was a good idea. It meant, among other things, that the rings had collectability value. And it was possible to control who obtained a ring to some extent. The biggest mistake was letting the Elves get hold of three. The other possessors weren't a problem, given the general greediness of Dwarves and the indescribable greed, corruption, and general pigheadedness of Men.

And yet ...

I have to wonder.

Losing the One Ring was a serious disaster, the implications of which are still being felt on our side. I can't think for the life of me where it went to. We knew Isildur took it. We knew he was ambushed. It should have been found on his body. But it disappeared, and that's been bothering me lately. Somehow it seems as if the One Ring has become and more and more essential to our plans. Of course, it's possible that if we'd been left alone a bit longer in Dol Guldur—I'll have some extremely strong words for that wizard when we catch up to him—we could have compensated for that to a degree. But as always in this world, it's rush, rush, rush.

The Dark Forces of Middle-earth have a good deal to be proud of in the Rings of Power. There's no question they gave value for money. The Nazgûl alone are probably worth the price. But I can't help feeling that there's something we've overlooked ...

Well, I'm sure it will come to me later.

One of the most ridiculous charges laid against the Dark Tower and what it stands for is that it created Orcs.

Really? That's supposed to be a bad thing?

It's not as if there's something unethical about creating races. Hellooooo! Elves? Orcs were a reasonable and just solution to the problem of Elven oppression. Elves had been swanking about the continent as if they owned it, having everything their own way, never asking anybody else for advice or assistance. So Orcs were intended to balance things out a bit.

In fact, the creation of Orcs accomplished several things.

1. **It provided a ready-made army.** As I said earlier, if you're trying to conquer a place and hold it without an army, you're just spinning your wheels.

2. **It gave the Elves something to do.** Idle hands are a Balrog's workshop, as the saying goes. The Elves, sunk as they were in a permanent state of sloth, needed something to stir them up. Sometimes people need an enemy to fight against.

3. **They're replaceable and therefore make ideal workers.** Want the path to the Chambers of Fire on Mount Doom kept clean and swept? Send some Orcs. Want to build a watchtower on a high peak in the Mountains of Shadow? Send some Orcs. Want to pick up a few trespassers for questioning? Send some Orcs. If a few of them get lost along the way, it's no problem; just make some more. Elves, Dwarves, and Men, on the other hand (I don't know about halflings) take a ridiculously long time to reproduce.

It's true, as some have complained, that an Orc's bodily hygiene probably could use some adjusting, but slaughtering villages all day is hard work. Who would begrudge an Orc a bit of honest sweat on its brow? It's also true that they're quarrelsome and sometimes seem to kill as many of each other as of the enemy, but that's simply the result of inadequate training. The squads of Orcs that guard the Dark Tower are orderly and obedient—and any of them who aren't are weeded out pretty quickly and disposed of.

So, we come back to the central point. Order. Law and order. Is that really such a bad thing for Middle-earth? Isn't that what all of us, in our own ways, have been aiming for all along?

I suppose some of it could have been accomplished with a bit less bloodshed, but in order to make an omelet you have to break a few eggs; you might even have to hurl them against a stone wall and watch their yolks shatter and run down the stones. Personally, I prefer a bit of bloodshed now to rivers of blood later as some new alliance of Elves, Men, Dwarves, halflings, and every other race that comes doddering out of the woodwork tries to disrupt everything in Middle-earth for their own ends.

At a minimum, it would be perfectly possible to draw up a peace agreement that would benefit both sides in the coming conflict. We get everything up to the Anduin, and the Lords of the West get everything else (if they're going to be "Lords of the West," after all, the least they can do is *stay* in the West). That's a very fair arrangement, and we'll be putting it forth at the earliest opportunity. But will it be accepted? Based on my previous experience, all I can say is, don't hold your breath.

Failing that, it looks as if the only solution is going to be war. I want to stress that we didn't want this war. It was in no way our fault. If we'd had our way, things would have turned out much differently.

But, as I said at the beginning, the whole thing really started with Morgoth.

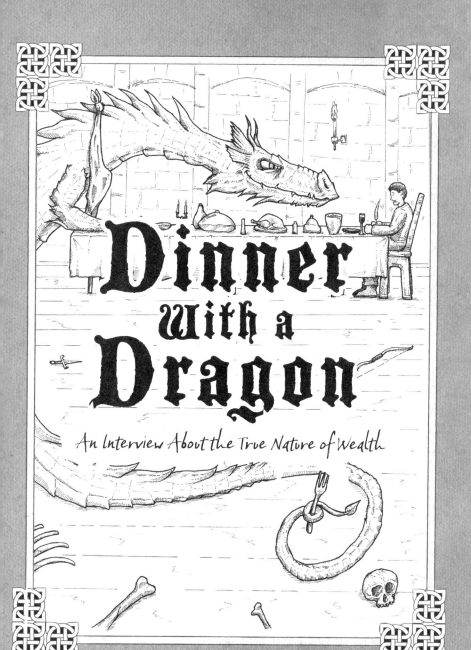

Dinner with a Dragon

An Interview About the True Nature of Wealth

O ragons steal gold and jewels, you know, from men and elves and dwarves, wherever they can find them; and they guard their plunder as long as they live (which is practically forever, unless they are killed), and never enjoy a brass ring of it. Indeed they hardly know a good bit of work from a bad, though they usually have a good notion of the current market value...

—From J.R.R. Tolkien's *The Hobbit*

This is a story about the time I set out to interview a fearsome dragon that had taken up residence in a mountainside castle that once belonged to a kingdom of Dwarves. The dragon had been there for many years, and the surrounding landscape had been reduced to a scorched and uninhabited wasteland. I felt this creature must have a story to tell, and I wanted to report it to the world.

The evening began with a climb up the side of the mountain. The crumbled old castle that clung to the hillside was my destination. It was home to a fearsome dragon that had taken up residence decades ago after raining fire and destruction down upon the place. The inhabitants had long since fled, and the dragon hoarded their gold and jewels along with other treasures that he'd pillaged from neighboring villages and towns.

I couldn't help noticing the lack of vegetation as I made my way along the winding rocky path that led to the place. The dragon's fire had laid waste to the trees and fauna, and despite the passing of many years, nothing grew.

Upon reaching the castle I knocked four times, as instructed by my editor. I then entered and announced myself, also as instructed. I then found the stone staircase that led to the depths of the dungeon beneath the place, where the dragon had made its sleeping chambers. As I reached the bottom of the steps, I found myself in a cavernous space with a vaulted ceiling. The dragon was curled up, much like a lapdog, on piles and piles of gold. The smell of the creature was nearly overpowering—a truly noxious odor. I thought he might be sleeping, so I introduced myself again. He quickly but politely corrected me. He had been aware of my presence before I'd even ascended the mountainside.

The dragon slid down from his mound of gold and approached me. After looking me over, he invited me to sit at one end of a long table, where a chair and place setting was laid out for me. He settled down at the other end. A couple of small goblins came with serving trays and laid out filled bowls and overflowing plates before us. I tucked into some very tender cutlets of meat simmered in a delectable sauce. The dragon ignored my inquiry as to what we were eating and changed the subject to our interview—the purpose of my visit. What follows is my faithful attempt to transcribe our conversation.

***

Gracious Dragon, thank you for inviting me into your home. I'd heard stories of foreboding, but I must say, I love what you've done with the place.

Dear boy, you are too kind. It's good to have a visitor. My Orc friends are rather poor conversationalists. All they seem to want to talk about is viscera.

Striking fear into the hearts of so many tends to make one lonely, so I'm very glad for the company. And as long as you don't try to wander off with any of my gold in your pockets, we'll get along just fine.

So tell me, what would you like to know?

Resplendent Dragon, it's interesting that you should mention the loneliness. That's part of my intended line of inquiry. I'd very much like to know what keeps you in this den of solitude. Your power is legendary, so why stay here?

Well, I have my treasure and all of my things. There's a lot of history behind each and every golden trinket you see here. I love shiny things, but I love how I came by them even more. I know each piece of gold in this place intimately and remember the story behind each and every ruby, diamond, and sapphire.

Your wealth is truly legendary. Do you have any advice for those who might seek financial guidance from someone who has achieved your level of success?

You have to be aggressive. You can't sit around counting your scales and expect diamonds to fall into your lap. And once you have your treasure, you should defend it tooth and nail. That is the way of things.

With all due respect, your opulence, what is it about dragons and gold?

The true allure of gold is in its history. It's in the changing of hands. It's in the scandal, the murder, and the betrayal that is wed to the stuff. Oh, the stories and memories this pile behind me could tell if it were able.

There were screams, believe you me. Do you see this cup? This is the cup of an Elf king who is now but a cold cinder. I still remember the look on his face as he took his last sip of wine from it before seeing the shadow of my wings envelope his kingdom.

So it's not really about the money?

Well, the money is nice. But look around. I don't have a lot of overhead here. I mean, what am I going to spend it on? And if I need more, I can just take it from someone else. So, no ... I guess it's not really about the money. But wealth is a relative thing. This wealth means a great deal to me, not because of its worth but because of the thrill of taking it from some poor schmuck.

Evil is pretty much my thing. After all, I'm a dragon.

Aren't there good dragons?

Pshaw. Mere lizards, that lot.

So what gives you meaning in life, brilliant Dragon?

That's a pretty grand question, my boy. Let me see if I can articulate this. The world is an oyster, as they say. I believe you have to get out there and take the things you want in life. Let's say you want a magic sword with an ornate golden hilt, a chest filled with heirloom jewelry, or just a nice plump pony for snacking on. Well, sitting around wishing for those things doesn't do you a bit of good. You have to swoop in there, all wings and flames, and take those things. Then it becomes not about the things you wanted. It becomes about being magnificent.

That's quite a philosophy.

It's made me the wyrm I am today.

Magnificent and benevolent Dragon, isn't there more to life than treasure?

Oh my dear boy, of course there is. Haven't you been listening? There's adventure and luxury and the thrill of the hunt.

There's nothing like flying over a mountaintop and swooping down on a village of people running and hiding in fear of you. It's flattering and exhilarating. All of those people whose towns I destroyed mean so very much to me. It's an intimate thing to destroy someone's home. Those people and I are inexorably linked. I've changed their lives forever, and the ones who lived to see another day will fear me until they take their last breath. Some people say that the closest you can be to someone is to be a friend or lover—I would argue that sworn enemies are more passionate.

When one considers what is true richness in life, one must think of the whole of one's experiences. I've tasted things that are at their truest, rawest, and ripest. That is true richness.

What do you invest in?

I'm guessing you mean financial investment. I'll tell you right now, I don't believe in it. I put it all under the mattresses, as the saying goes. The pile lies all around me. I'm not looking to gain interest—that has no value to me. The gains I make are linked to experience, as I pointed out before.

If you're looking to invest in something, invest in yourself. Invest in experience. At the end of the day, all you have is yourself and your memories, really.

That's very profound for someone who is so ... can I say "evil?"

Oh yes! Go ahead and say it. So many take offense, but I do not. Words only have the power that you give them, you know. Someone says that someone or something is evil, and it's supposed to be a bad thing. But you know what? Everyone I ever met that is supposedly evil is powerful. Everyone I met that is supposedly evil is successful. Sure, those individuals were out for themselves, but you know what else you can call that? Honest. Anyone who says that they aren't out for themselves first and foremost is a liar. Sure, you can tell yourself that you're being selfless and that your actions are purely philanthropic, but you have to realize that what you're doing in that instance is rationalization. You are likely thinking that if you do this selfless thing, you're a good person, and the universe will owe you one and look out for you, or that you'll go to the Undying Lands when you die or some other such nonsense. Well, guess what? You can't barter with destiny.

So you don't believe in a higher power?

> Sure I do. And that power is me. I'm a dragon. Look
> at these magnificent wings. Feel the inferno of my
> breath. Hear the thunder of my thumping tail. See
> the gleam of my talons. I command my own destiny.
> I decide my future.

**Forgive me, magnificent Dragon, but that sounds a bit lonely.
What about relationships?**

> Are you and I not having a conversation now? Are we
> not forming a relationship this very moment? Your
> question is based on the idea that a relationship must
> be built on friendship to be of any worth. To me, re-
> lationships built on fear and hatred are much more
> satisfying. They are more honest and real.

Fearsome Dragon, you are truly beginning to frighten me.

> Really? That's so nice of you to say. Flattery will get
> you everywhere, dear boy.

No, seriously. You're quite scary.

> Well, you're doing a fine job here yourself. These are
> thought-provoking questions. Very top notch.

Well, thank you.

> You're quite welcome. How are you enjoying the meal?

It's fantastic. What is this delectable dish?

> I'm going to keep that to myself, I'm afraid. I will tell
> you that the real secret is in the sauce. It's a béarnaise.

Well, it's wonderful. Have you always been such a foodie?

You know, in my youth I would eat pretty much anything and not give it a thought. I ate sheep, horses, Dwarves ... I didn't care so much. But these days I find that food is really one of the great pleasures in life. It's like treasure that you can eat. Why settle for anything other than the finest?

When you look back on your life, what do you hope you will have accomplished?

Hope is such a wishy-washy word. I will look back and see all the change I've inflicted across the landscape and know all I've done: villages razed, forests decimated, fortresses in ruin, a pile of treasure in my basement. All of those things are evidence of the life I've lived. There is no such thing as hope; only what I will have done and the proof that I have done it.

Is there any other kind of life for you? Any other purpose or vocation you might have pursued?

Hmm. You know, I always was interested in journalism.

Umm ... are you serious?

Oh yes. It's one of the reasons I agreed to this interview. What do you think? Could I be an intrepid reporter like you? Are there any openings at your publication? I was thinking maybe I could have a regular byline, you know, an advice column or something along those lines.

And with that, our interview was over. I shook the dragon's talon and made my way back down the hillside thinking of the sadness of this creature who was so convinced of the nobleness of his self-imposed isolation. Sure he was evil, but did he deserve to be left all alone like that? It bothered me for some reason. I resolved to help the dragon. Perhaps I would help him find a job.

The Art of Sneakiness

Sir:

*In searching the battlefield for the dead and reliev-
ing them of their weapons—serviceable weapons,
that is—a work detail found the enclosed manuscript. It is evidently a guide of some kind passed
out by the Enemy to their troops to guide them,
should they find themselves behind our lines. It
may prove immensely valuable in detecting signs
of enemy saboteurs and spies, and I suggest that
its contents be analyzed and copies made and distributed to all unit commanders.*

Respectfully,

—R

(*First portion of manuscript burnt*)

... extreme caution in approaching anyone. For this reason, you
are advised to avoid contact until you have assembled a convincing backstory that you can bring out if necessary. You are also advised to be aware of the cultural backgrounds of various enemies,
to which end, the following is presented:

ELVES

Elves generally can be found in wooded areas, because they have
an unwholesome attachment to trees and shrubs. They are tall, thin,
and irritatingly smug. On the other hand, they are generally shrewd-
er than other races that have allied themselves against us, so they
should not be underestimated.

Elves have an extensive knowledge of the lore of Middle-earth, including all sorts of "wise" sayings and bits of idiotic verse about Middle-earth history. If you encounter an Elf and want to engage its attention, have a tale or two handy about tragic Elf maidens who fall in love with mortals and spend centuries lamenting their beloveds and letting tears drop that turn into flowers. ... That sort of thing comes easily enough once you put your mind to it, even if it makes you throw up a little in your mouth.

Another thing that Elves are interested in is their own history—they're the most narcissistic of the races of Middle-earth. They can never hear too much about where they came from, how much Eru loved them, and the great tragedy (as they conceive it) of their love for Middle-earth, which they must, alas, alas, alas, leave forever. Yes, they really do go on like that.

Spend a little time studying Elvish history (nauseating, I know, but necessary if you're going to make a good impression), so you'll be able to spit out some facts or a chunk of one of their old tales, allowing you to be accepted as an Elf Friend, the highest accolade accorded non-Elves.

Elves are expert archers and are mildly good with swords, but in general they are much better at attacking their enemies at a distance while remaining safe behind battlements, trees, or anything else that provides shelter. When faced with a full-on frontal attack, they're more inclined to give way and, in all likelihood, will wind up in one of the scattered companies that are mooning about Middle-earth, waiting to leave. This is one of the great mysteries about Elves: If they're bound and determined to leave Middle-earth, why don't they simply head for the Grey Havens and not let the door hit their skinny butts on the way out? But no, they have to spend hundreds of years bemoaning the fact that they're leaving the place they love and making up songs and poetry about it.

Sneaking up on Elves isn't very easy; they know a lot of wood-craft, since they're in touch with trees and everything. The best approach to attacking the Elf folk is probably treachery. Even there, you're likely to run into trouble, since Elves can "see into your eyes and detect the evil dwelling in your soul." From that standpoint, don't stand too close to an Elf, and whatever you do, don't look it in the eye.

DWARVES

Dwarves are short, egotistical, demanding, drunk, and mostly stupid. The way to get behind a Dwarf is to throw a gold coin ahead of him. The way to make friends with a Dwarf is to offer him a contract to mine coal. The way to get a Dwarf to do something that's against his self-interest is to offer him a drink. Keep offering drinks until you run out of money or he runs out of gut. A word of caution: The former is likely to happen a long time before the latter.

Elves are convinced of their innate superiority because they were once important. Dwarves, never having been important, argue their superiority on the basis of attitude. They insist that at some point in the past they *must* have been important and therefore should be treated with respect. You can see how well that's gone over.

The really important thing about Dwarves, from our point of view, is how easily they can be corrupted. You can sway their allegiance for an astonishingly low amount of money. Add into this that they simply hate, hate, *HATE* Elves and can be moved into any course of action if you suggest that it's one the Elves don't want them to take, and we have a picture of a people who are the absolute last word when it comes to pliability.

In general, the Dwarves are a bit like the Elves in that they're primarily focused on their ancestors. Dwarves (and Elves) believe that one's worth is counted by the importance of one's forebears. For this reason, effective sneakiness among the Dwarves depends on constructing a believable family tree. The main houses one should attempt to establish an alliance to are:

1. **Durin.** This is the big one, "Durin the Deathless," (although he did eventually die).
2. **Borin.** The great-great-great-great-great-great-great grandson of Durin. I know that's a lot of greats.
3. **Thrór.** This is the grandfather of that prize troublemaker Thorin Oakenshield.

As long as you can claim some relationship to one of these three houses, you'll probably be trusted—insofar as the Dwarves trust anyone. The real way to win Dwarvish trust is to drink them all under the table.

MEN

It's common knowledge that Men are among the easiest of the mortal races to fool. They tend to be overly trusting and blind except in regards to matters of short-term self-interest. If you can maneuver one of them around, he's always ripe for a quick stab in the back. It's like loosing arrows at fish in a barrel.

To get a Man to do what you want, offer him:

1. **Gold.** If there's one thing calculated to turn a mortal's head, it's some of the heavy yellow stuff the Dwarves dig out of the ground in giant lumps. Melted, solid, hammered into something shiny—it doesn't matter as long as it's gold.
2. **Jewels.** The best kind are made by Elves, but diamonds, rubies, emeralds, sapphires, and anything else that glitters will work as well. Set a couple of them in a gold or silver tiara and the average Man won't be able to resist.
3. **Magic artifacts.** Magic to humans is like catnip to a cat: They can't resist it. It's rumored that He snared nine of them a long time ago with magic rings. You might not be able to use rings, but anything else that smacks of magic or looks as though it ought to be magic will probably bring a few Men sniffing around.
4. **Power.** If none of the above works, try power. Political office seems to be something that Men crave above anything else. Hard to say why, really, since for the most part it means a lot of responsibility, hard work, and dealing with the fact that everyone is angry with you most of the time, but there's no accounting for taste.

Men, like Elves, are proud of their lineage, so it's always possible to pose as a long-lost ancestor from a cadet branch of some sort. For all of their silliness, Men have a suspicious nature—a characteristic that you can use to your advantage, since it makes them ripe for manipulation. Much of the success of the agents of darkness over the past millennia has been gained by setting Men against each other and sitting back to watch the results. No other race is so good at self-destruction.

HALFLINGS

This is a race that's just come to the attention of this department. Ordinarily it wouldn't be worth spending time on such an insignificant people, but Higher Ups feel they have some unnamed role to play in forthcoming events, so we've done a bit of research about the best ways to approach them.

They're a short people—shorter than the Dwarves, even—and are largely confined to an area in the north called The Shire. They rarely venture out of their own lands, which is why no one in the rest of Middle-earth had heard of them until recently. They wear bright clothing, which makes them admirable targets for archers, even at a distance. They have large, hairy feet and they enjoy eating, drinking, and smoking a noxious substance called "pipe-weed," to which they're much addicted.

Since most halflings are credulous even by the standards of the West, they aren't difficult to fool. Tell a halfling you've got dinner waiting for him just over the hill, and he'll follow you in a quick minute, as soon as he has a chance to brush his toes and put on a fresh vest. Tell him that the dinner includes a barrel of ale and three desserts, and he won't even stop to do these things.

The one thing to notice about halflings is that they have the ability to move very quietly. For this reason, use only the best trackers on their trails and try, insofar as it is possible, to force them into the open. Once a halfling enters a wooded area, he's lost to us until he emerges, especially if he knows someone's looking for him.

THE TOOLS OF SNEAKING

It's been truly said that the greatest peril comes from the smallest sources. This is particularly true of covert operations. A large-scale movement against the enemy is likely to attract unpleasant attention, whereas a small, patient operation, often lasting many months or even years, can yield substantial and even decisive results. This section outlines the main tools of such operations and their expected results.

Message Interception

Covering the enemy's mail is among the most venerable spying tactics. You should always know what your enemy is up to, and opening his mail gives you a great deal of insight. Remember, *under no circumstances should the target be aware that his messages have been intercepted and read.*

If the mail is carried in traditional form, the operation is simple. An agent is planted within the postal service in a position in which he can intercept letters to and from the target. A pot of steaming water and a candle for melting wax seals are the only equipment required. Note that it is essential, if a seal is used, that the agent have an exact copy of the target's seal so the letters can be resealed after they have been copied. Letters should never be delayed more than a day.

If a messenger will hand carry the letter, greater sneakiness is required. It's possible to open and read the letter while the messenger is asleep (and sleep can always be enhanced by drugs; the halfling pipe-weed is admirable for this purpose).

In some circumstances, it may be necessary to stage a diversion lasting long enough for the message to be read. A rockslide, a sudden attack by bandits, a forest fire that frightens the messenger's horse—these are all acceptable. Again, whenever possible, reseal the letter once it has been read and return it to the messenger (in the case of a bandit attack, this may not be possible).

(*Note: At this point, several pages of the manuscript appear to be missing.*)

... for carrying of messages, see Appendix B, Crebain Information Agency.

Trash Detail

Humans and Dwarves have a tendency to throw away important documents as well as other useful intelligence assets. It is therefore recommended that whenever possible their middens be placed under surveillance and subject to regular review. Orcs are best suited to this duty, though they must be provided with exceedingly clear instructions concerning the material for which they are looking, as well as a warning to avoid eating anything that strikes their fancy. It is usually sufficient to tell them to collect all documents, no matter how trivial. Among the documents they should be on the lookout for are:

1. Army inventory lists
2. Battle plans
3. Personnel rosters, including the command structure of the enemy army
4. Weapons instruction manuals
5. Grocery lists

Any of these can mean the difference between victory and defeat.

Infiltration

Infiltrating the enemy, or providing intelligence boots on the ground, is without question the most important, as well as the most difficult, source of intelligence. For obvious reasons, infiltration must be undertaken by humans or Dwarves. Orcs are incapable of subtlety and deception and in any case would be peppered with arrows long before they could get within a hundred feet of an intelligence target. Elves cannot be turned to our side—we've certainly made attempts to do so. Humans, on the other hand, are bought off with promises of gold or power, while gold alone is usually sufficient for Dwarves.

Our most successful attempt to date in this regard has been [Note: name is smudged and illegible], who returned considerable intelligence to us before he was revealed. In typical human fashion, he was "mercifully" exiled from court, which meant a pointless wandering existence for several months until one of our companies of Orcs took pity on him and put a knife in his ribs.

A live intelligence asset must be highly trained and able to dissemble at a moment's notice. He must have an excellent cover story, that is to say, an explanation of why he is where he is. In the case of [name smudged again], who infiltrated a royal court, he was able to convince the king that he was a worthy counselor and establish a clear background of service in many other areas of the royal bureaucracy. This was a particularly high-profile case and quite unusual. In the normal course of things, it is much more likely that intelligence sources (called "moles" by some) can penetrate some secure bureaucratic post and remain there for years if need be.

Such "moles" are to be serviced by a case officer, who will report to the head of the intelligence service. Their reports are to be subject to extremely careful handling. In ideal circumstances, communication will be by *palantir*, but since very few of these are still functional and in our possession, this is unlikely to be an option.

For such a "mole," the goal should be maximum access with minimal exposure. That is to say, avoid taking a prominent part in anything, but find the best possible place from which to observe the enemy. Case officers should be ruthless in their handling of moles. If it is a choice between sacrificing the mole or sacrificing exposure, the dedicated officer will unhesitatingly choose the former.

Equipment

Agents in all areas of intelligence collection should have with them at all times the following:

- A dagger

- A parchment and writing materials

- Secret ink (fashioned from lemon juice, which turns brown when exposed to heat)

- A small vial of poison, to be taken if exposure is imminent

Note that in the past, agents have been reluctant to use their poison vials. Please be aware that the Dark Tower regards such behavior as a disturbing sign of disobedience and has ordered that any agent who returns to our ranks after being exposed will be interrogated by Him with predictable results.

WEAPONS FOR SNEAKING

It should go without saying that some weapons are better adapted to sneaking. The following section briefly considers the ideal weapons to be employed in an effective sneak.

Daggers

Remarkably versatile weapons, daggers are small, easily concealed, and can be used for stabbing, slashing, or throwing. Their greatest drawback is that they are not instantly lethal; an opponent hit in the stomach with a dagger is not going to fall over dead—he'll merely pull out the weapon, growl a bit, and come after you with renewed anger, at least until he bleeds to death.

Stilettos

These are a bit sharper and quieter than daggers. Victims don't tend to scream when stabbed with a stiletto—at least not very much. A stiletto can be quietly slipped between the fourth and fifth rib at a slight upward angle to penetrate the heart and cause instant death with no more than a minute or two of convulsing. With a stiletto, avoid the overhand backstab, since it tends to hit bone and break the blade. The stiletto, in other words, is made for delicate, intimate work. If possible, employ it immediately after an intimate act.

Garrotes

The key to effective garroting is that it must be unexpected. The victim should be thinking along the lines of, "Whoa! I was so thinking this was going to be a sword thrust from the front! This is so unexpected. I wonder what happens ne—"

A garrote should be slim, no more than a quarter-inch thick in order to effectively cut off air supply. It can be concealed around your wrist until needed and should have knots at each end to assist grip. There are two alternatives in method: over the head or around the neck. Over the head is preferred by professionals, but amateurs are advised to avoid it, since the garrote has a tendency to be caught on the target's nose. Instead, the rope should be thrown swiftly but gently around the neck and immediately pulled tight. Be ready, as the victim will most likely thrash about before expiring.

Axe

Axes are large, heavy, and messy, but one can't deny that they get the job done. One good swing and the target's head goes bouncing down the walk with its tongue sticking out. The problem lies in striking before the victim is aware of what's going on. This is why the ideal position for an axe wielder is behind the victim (approximately a foot and a half away). The ideal setting is a dark night with a single bright light shining on the target's neck. The assassin should also be somewhat taller than his target, since the most deadly blows are delivered from slightly above; the operative may want to consider putting lifts in his boots before striking.

Axes also require cleaning; a conscientious user will wipe the weapon clean and pay special attention to the areas where the handle joins the blade to avoid pesky bloodstains later on.

Bow and Arrow

Bluff old traditionalists prefer to stick to the tried and true: the arrow loosed from fifty feet away, preferably from a tree. A bow is, in many respects, the ideal weapon. It is silent, deadly, easy to master, and capable of wounding or killing, depending on the user's preference. Arrows can be barbed or laced with poison, and, in extreme circumstances, a thin rope can be attached to the arrow, enabling the attacker to yank on it and topple the target off the top of a battlement. The chief drawback of the weapon lies in the need to constantly replenish the supply of ammunition. It's possible to reuse arrows, but their shelf life is generally three or four kills. Arrows must also be adjusted for balance, fletching, and so forth, all of which require specialized skills that may not be available in the field.

Clubs

Clubs are not generally used in assassinations or in acts of sneakiness, since they're large, loud (the noise of a club hitting someone's skull resounds for some distance), and one runs the risk of missing on the first blow. They're generally the preferred weapons of trolls and the less subtle races, but that shouldn't stop others from appreciating their effectiveness. An Elf who is hit in the head with a six-foot club will generally stay down, at least for a while (and can be dispatched conveniently with some other weapon). An expertly employed club can silence a watchman with a single blow and, in a skirmish, can knock out several opponents at once. It can also be used to block stray arrows, trip opponents, and smash in doors. When it comes down to it, this weapon is traditional but highly effective. Don't count it out.

SNEAKING

Finally, a few words about sneaking—the art of not being seen. It's not as easy as one might think. In Moria, for instance—

(*Note: Several pages of the manuscript here are obliterated with a combination of soot, fire, and blood.*)

—caves present admirable opportunities for concealment. However, and this cannot be stressed enough, in a cave, every sound is echoed and re-echoed. Only sneak into a cave if you're confident of being extremely quiet.

Water

Water is an effective method of concealing one's tracks. Running streams are better than rivers, as rivers form barriers that can't be easily crossed. However, if you must deal with a river, seek out pieces of driftwood and float along the surface, if possible by night, until you arrive at a likely place to come ashore.

When traveling by stream, avoid displacing stones and rocks, as these can provide clues for trackers. If trees border the stream, it may be possible to travel through the trees instead by jumping from branch to branch for a time to prevent leaving tracks.

Don't remain with the stream too long or you risk being pulled downstream and out of your way.

Plains

Plains and open areas are the hardest to sneak in, since they provide little or no shelter. They're best traversed at night and with great caution. If you must cross in daylight, it's probably best to throw caution to the winds. Wear an ominous black cloak and ride a black horse. If people are going to see you—and they probably are—you might as well scare the living daylights out of them. At least that way they'll leave you alone to do your sneaking in peace. They may even go out of their way to avoid you.

The great advantage of plains is that they provide an opportunity for speed. Don't hold back. Spur the horse (or whatever you're riding) to a gallop. Remember, if you can see your enemies, they can see you, so there's no point in trying to conceal your presence. Set your sights on a forest or tower or some place in the distance that offers the possibility of concealment and go all out. Whatever you do, don't turn and fight. Because you're under the open sun, your enemy has the advantage.

A FEW FINAL WORDS

Sneaking requires finesse above all. If it could be accomplished by brute force, we'd send Orcs to do it. Or trolls. But in its essence, sneakiness should be quiet and subtle. Although there are some races that should be simply killed on sight—Elves, for instance—for the most part, our enemies should be turned, confused, or at most knocked on the head or left for drunk to sleep it off. (As noted before, the halflings' narcotic pipe-weed has underdeveloped possibilities, and a branch of our Research and Development team is hard at work on—

(Note: At this point the manuscript breaks off. A note, scribbled on the final page in scrawling letters, reads, "Recalled to the Dark Tower. Will finish this lat—" One can only speculate on the fate of the author. This should be of immense importance to us in preparing for the upcoming war. I pass it along with my recommendation that it be studied with the utmost intensity.)

A always
B be
C casting

Habits
for
Highly Effective
Dark Wizards

First, let me make it perfectly clear that whatever Elvish chronicles and so on may say about Good triumphing in the end and Evil consuming itself, dark wizards are not only more effective than white wizards—they're way cooler. I should know—having seen both sides first hand, so to speak.

For a start, just look at the standard dark wizard's robe. At first glance it looks white, doesn't it? But take another look: You can see every color of the rainbow. This reflects a fundamental fact about dark wizards: They're nothing if not versatile. They change and adapt. White wizards merely plod along the straight and narrow, muttering to themselves about the fate of the world and the strength of an enemy that can be overcome by the smallest foe. Don't be fooled. The fact that their robes are white has nothing to do with the purity of their intentions. It just makes them show up better against a shadowy background so some enterprising archer can take a shot at them.

Dark wizards, on the other hand, can creep along unseen until their opposition becomes completely trusting and unsuspecting. And then ... *wham!* They're down and out before they know what's hit them.

If you're looking to begin a career in the dark arts, or if you simply covet that corner office and some goody-two-shoes is standing between you and the glory of corporate domination, you'll find these guidelines for being an effective Evil Overlord quite useful. Others may add to this list, though I wouldn't recommend you ask them; they might think you were taking a liberty and have you for breakfast. Or lunch. Or tea.

TEN THINGS TO ALWAYS DO
IF YOU'RE AN EVIL OVERLORD

1. **Be mysterious.** Everyone likes a bit of mystery. If you're out there in the open, constantly mingling with the proles, where's the fun in that for them? This is a case of "less is more." To really build legendary status, I recommend only showing up two or three times a century. And when you do show up, some bells and whistles—or in this case, smoke and fireworks—are probably indicated. Leave your audience with the smell of sulphur in their clothing. It takes days to wash out, and it'll remind them of your awful presence. Some minor burns and scars can help this along as well.

   Don't make any clear or straightforward pronouncements. It's far better to leave your followers with enough ambiguity to keep them debating your proclamations for months or even years after your departure. With luck, you can make them vague enough to keep opposing factions burning each other's adherents as heretics. Then, when you show up again after a century, you can straighten everything out just before giving another set of confusing instructions. This sort of thing keeps your minions on their toes.

2. **Don't be afraid to use up minions.** Remember, they're expendable, but you're not. In any dangerous situation, the rule is "minions first." If, during a battle, your strategy requires the temporary distraction of a hopeless charge against an entrenched position, well, that's what foot soldiers are for.

   To this point, it's important as an Evil Overlord that you have a reliable source of minions. Most overlords just make them, usually in some sort of assembly line. A few have tried recruiting, sending minions with sandwich boards into villages ("See the world! Join the forces of Evil! Slaughter millions and gratify your psychopathic impulses!") However, manufacturing works better.

It's also helpful to have some specialization among minions. For instance, there are spying/tracking minions (usually with big ears and noses); fighting minions (large stature, long arms, occasional body piercings); and work-a-day minions for fetching the morning coffee, cooking dinner, and torturing prisoners (small, servile, and with soft voices).

Above all, remember that nothing demonstrates your absolute power and ruthlessness like publicly murdering a few minions, chosen at random. For some reason, people are more apt to fear you if you show no compunction about killing creatures that are supposed to be on your side. Don't worry about being wasteful—when you kill minions, you send the implied message that you've got so many that you can afford to dispose of a few.

3. **Get an army.** No one respects you unless you have soldiers at your command who are willing to die for you. The bigger the army, the more respect you'll get. Size matters.

The biggest problem with an army is that you have to feed, clothe, and equip it. Here's another time when minions come in handy. Set them to banging out swords, shields, helmets, siege towers, catapults, and so on. Feeding can be a bigger problem. If your army is composed of meat eaters (and it probably should be), you can sustain it on a steady diet of minions, especially those who are tired after a long day of forging weapons of war. But the most important lesson here is that you need to put the army to work.

To that end, don't create your army until you have something for it to attack. Of course, you can give it practice by sending it to raid local villages, terrorize the countryside, and so forth, but you need something big for it to attack: a city to besiege or another army to defeat. Once you've dispatched it on its task, maintaining its food supply is no longer your problem.

4. **Make your magic terrifying.** White wizards are inclined to waste their magical gifts on stupid things like fireworks, casting out demons, and starting stubborn campfires. But why waste your efforts on such frivolity? Magic should be used to scare the pants off people. The best kind involves very loud explosions with lots of fire, smoke, raining cinders, mountains blowing up, and so on. If you can use your magic to raise an army of the dead, that's good, too. Not only is such an army scary, it's also indestructible. The only downside is that if the army gets out of control, it's liable to turn on you, but that's a small price to pay, especially if you have plenty of minions and soldiers standing between you and the dead army.

Weather magic can be useful as well. If your enemy is trying to cross a high mountain pass, dump some snow and rocks on them. If you can conjure it from a distance, you'll stymie them at no cost to yourself. Avalanches can accomplish much the same purpose. If the enemy is crossing a deep valley, bring on a disastrous storm and flood.

When used correctly, weather magic can scar the land for a long time and put up natural defenses around you. Of course, you can achieve much the same effect by defoliating everything in sight and spreading out shallow pools covered in oily scum and filled with half-living creatures that will bite the flesh off the ankles of anyone stupid enough to wade through them.

Death and destruction is the general aim of your magic. Remember, Evil Overlords don't go in for cheery gardens filled with happy bunnies and garden gnomes and brightly blooming blossoms that spread the scent of lemon and honey on a gentle breeze. In an Evil Overlord's garden, the grass has been rooted up and replaced with jagged rocks, the flowers are dead, the predominant smells are of rotting flesh, and the bunnies are roasting on a spit over an open fire.

The gnomes, however, are still in place.

5. **Ally yourself with animals.** But not just any animals: large, terrifying ones with lots of sharp teeth, pointy tusks, and glowing red eyes. Ones that roam around in packs at night and greet travelers with low growls and a query about what part of them tastes best.

Some animals that are especially useful to have on your side include:

   a. *Wolves.* These come in several sizes; you want the large, economy model. Not only are they fierce fighters, but they can also serve as mounts for your smaller soldiers. Of course, you'll have to train the wolves not to eat their riders, but doing so shouldn't cost you more than a few dozen soldiers. Wolves naturally hunt in packs and love the taste of blood—especially that of Elves, Dwarves, humans, and wizards.

   b. *Bears.* They can fight upright, they tower over most opponents, and, most important, they can climb trees.

Their big problem is that they're rather slow moving, but in force they are almost unstoppable.

c. *Spiders.* They're territorial and practically useless when there aren't any trees around (although not always; sometimes they make their lairs in caves). On the other hand, there are a lot of them—one spider mommy has lots of babies—and they can immobilize the unwary, hanging their prey in webs for your convenient collection. If you've got a tower (see below), they make good guardians. For feeding of your spiders, see the previous section on minions.

d. *Kraken.* Obviously this creature can't live out of water, but it's tremendously effective, even at a short distance from its pool, because of its long, snake-like arms. Even if some irritating adventurer cuts a few of these appendages off, the kraken will keep attacking and will, given time, grow back the severed limbs. All in all, a most useful creature to have on your side.

e. *Giant flying lizards with big pointy teeth.* Great for practically anything. It almost seems overkill to give them riders, even if the riders are powerful sorcerers and can slay anything that gets in their paths. Your motto should be, "An Evil Overlord can never have too many flying lizards."

Overall, remember that animals are mostly loyal and practically maintenance free, since they find their own food source. Sending a pack of ravening wolves in the direction of a few villages can be an excellent way to spread terror and destruction through the countryside, while also keeping your soldiers on their toes.

6. **Build a tower.** Not just a little one, either, but a really, really *big* tower. We're talking overcompensation here. It's possible you may find an old tower you can move into. That's okay, provided it has a reputation for Evil—it must be haunted by the spirits of long-dead witch-kings, or something equally fearsome.

Ideally it should be located on top of a rocky crag, in the middle of a dark, sinister forest, or in the middle of a stark and frightening plain with a few twisted trees surrounding it. There should be wolves howling and possibly an approach over a long bridge with no rails that spans a bottomless crevice. (Note: A bottomless crevice is excellent for disposing of garbage, used-up minions, and hapless adventurers.) It should be crowned with spikes (or spiky-looking small towers) and have lots of narrow slits for windows, suitable for shooting arrows, pouring boiling oil, etc.

What it should *not* have is secret entrances, water ducts, air shafts, or other means of unseen penetration. There should be only *one* way in: through the front door. Which should be big, iron, studded with sharp nails, impossible to open from the outside without magic or a lot of assistance, and guarded by ten-foot-tall soldiers with snarling wolves. If anyone gets past them unseen, you deserve to be overthrown.

The tower should also contain dungeons, which should be deep underground, heavily guarded (see previous paragraph), lightless, and generally depressing. Never imprison anyone by putting them on top of the tower and leaving them there, unguarded, for weeks at a time, only checking on them occasionally to make sure they haven't jumped off the edge. That's just silly. You lose prisoners that way.

7. **Forge some magic weapons.** If you don't have magical abilities yourself, find someone who does and put him to work. You're going to need serious armaments if you want to rule the world—some stuff that will kill or maim large numbers of your opponents at once. Don't settle for something that kills them one at a time; we're talking about magical weapons of mass destruction here. Some things you should consider:

a. *Swords.* These are great, provided when you swing them you slay twenty of your foes with a single blow. One thing you never want to do is get into a sword fight with your greatest enemy, particularly a humble nobody from a village no one's ever heard of but who is Predestined by the Fates to Confront Evil Itself and vanquish it. If you encounter such a person, don't fight him yourself. Hang back and send your soldiers and minions in to dispose of the nuisance.

b. *Bows and arrows.* Handy for killing from a distance—always a good thing in combat—but they need greater destructive power than an ordinary weapon. Exploding arrows can come in handy, especially if you can manufacture them in quantity and equip your archers with them. There's nothing like sending a flight of arrows toward the enemy and blowing up their front line of infantry.

c. *Catapults.* These are essential in any siege, but they're twice as effective if they're magical. This will enable them to throw their missiles higher and farther, not to mention throwing flaming balls that will start fires in the besieged city. If you don't have magical catapults, settle for throwing the heads of enemies whom you've slain in battle.

d. *Crossbows.* Though cumbersome and harder to load than a regular bow and arrow, crossbows nonetheless shoot with far more force. You can construct magical bolts that will penetrate armor, wood, stone, or pretty much anything else that stands between you and the target at which you're shooting. Now all you need is something to stop people from shooting at you.

e. *Morning stars.* Spiked maces. Even an ordinary morning star can do quite a bit of damage. Imbue it with magical properties and it's deadly every time. Like the sword, the ideal magical morning star takes out legions of the enemy with each swing.

Other possible weapons include billhooks, pikes, daggers, glaives, war-hammers, battle-axes, quarterstaffs, maces, stilettos, dirks, battering rams, ballistae, and siege towers. Feel free to improvise.

8. **Get some magical armor.** It's not enough that you should be able to easily kill large numbers of your enemies in battle. It's equally important that none of them be able to kill you. Here's where magically enhanced armor is essential.

Of course, ordinary armor can lessen the damage done to you, but you don't want to take any chances. You may be standing behind the lines, directing the battle, planning your strategy, checking your messages, and suddenly some Elf archer gets ideas into his pointy head and takes a pot shot at you. Even in a full suit of plate armor, it's possible his arrow will find an unlucky chink.

To prevent this sort of unfortunate accident, read on:

a. *Leather armor.* No, no, no, no! Not for an Evil Overlord. No self-respecting leader of the forces of Darkness would consider putting on such a thing. Leather armor (made of boiled leather, by the way) might stop an arrow or two if you're lucky, but it won't stop much more than that. Leave leather armor to the soldiers in the front line, who are all going to get killed in the first ten minutes of the battle anyway, so it hardly matters what they're wearing. Leather armor is inexpensive, so use it only for your most expendable troops and never for yourself.

b. *Chain Mail.* Now we're getting a bit closer to serious armor, although chain mail is the sort of thing Dwarves wear, and who wants to be mistaken for a Dwarf? The big problem with chain mail is that even though it'll probably stop arrows and even some sword thrusts, its flexibility means it's useless against a blow from a morning star, and even a spear thrust can do quite a bit of harm, especially if the chain links are broken. Elves have chain mail as well, forged from *truesilver* or *mithril*. That's more like it, since it's practically unbreakable, but there's not much *mithril* around. Finding a few stray Elves and sticking their feet in a fire might be a useful start to finding some.

c. *Partial plate.* Good for the bits it covers, certainly. Usually this includes the chest, head, and possibly some of the leg. Of course, if anyone hits you in any other area, you're in trouble.

    d. *Full plate.* Now we're talking! Full, comprehensive coverage from head to toe. No possibility of a random blow from a sword getting through. All you need now is a bit of magical assistance.

Simple spell casting on full plate armor will ensure its immunity to pretty much all weapon attacks. Note that if you've poured most of your power into a magical artifact that you carry about with you—say, a ring—you should chiefly avoid the possibility that someone is going to cut off your ring finger and eventually destroy your power. From this standpoint, you might do well to consider wearing the ring on the inside of your armor rather than the outside. Just a suggestion.

9. **Subdue a land.** Everyone needs a base from which to operate. The best one for you is a rocky, barren, desert-like land with lots of mountains surrounding it and big, clear plains over which you can march your armies. Somewhere in it you need a place to grow food (or what passes for food as far as your soldiers and other minions are concerned) and plenty of space for you to erect your Tower (see above). Subdued lands, inconveniently, often come with indigenous populations, but you can easily turn them into slaves or engage in a little genocide to clear things for your organization. Most of your watchtowers and fortifications on the borders of the land should be turned inward; the point is less about preventing people from getting in (I mean, who really wants to get in?) and more about keeping them from getting out.

As a security measure, when patrols are moving through your land, make them remove their helmets, so you can easily recognize any intruders (Elves, Dwarves, hobbits) who may try to sneak in and start something. If there's a place that's the Source of Your Power in your land, mount a twenty-four-hour guard on it, no matter what else you may be doing. Preferably, surround it with soldiers, standing two or three deep—and awake and alert at all times. You can spare the soldiers. You can always make more.

The same thing is true of your tower, which should not be located smack dab in the middle of your land but rather in some quiet, obscure, out-of-the-way corner that's not easily accessible to casual visitors. After all, you're the supreme Evil Overlord. There's no need to be ostentatious about it.

10. **Ally yourself with a dragon.** The challenge of dragons is that they tend to have their own agendas. This makes them dangerous but effective allies. Dragons are some of the most venerable, dignified, and intelligent creatures in Middle-earth, and therefore this is one of the few times I recommend that you go see a dragon yourself instead of sending an underling. Dispatching minions to negotiate a treaty with a dragon is likely to result in a long line of minions reduced to their component parts and returned to you in baskets. A dragon requires that you meet him face to face.

Keep in mind that a dragon isn't going to do something for you without getting something in return. When you negotiate with a dragon, you enter a two-way street. Thus, begin negotiations with a clear idea of what you're prepared to offer. Fortunately, since dragons love treasure, you have a logical place to open. Start low and proceed to high. As a side offer, you may want to suggest that you'll deliver the treasure to the dragon with a couple of captive Dwarves, so he'll have something to snack on while he recounts his hoard.

TEN THINGS NEVER TO DO IF YOU'RE AN EVIL OVERLORD

1. **Don't put all of your power into one small object that is easily lost, stolen, or destroyed.** Spread your power around. Decentralized malice and evil is a lot harder to get rid of than that which is concentrated in one trinket. If you insist on putting your evil essence into physical objects, put it into many of them. And make those objects different. Don't, for instance, create a bunch of rings. Consider instead an array of ordinary household objects: The Salt Shaker of Unmentionable Peril, the Beer Glass of Impending Doom, the Garden Hose of Unspeakable Evil. That sort of thing.

Doing so will make it harder for your enemy to locate and destroy the sources of your power and will enhance the objects in which your evil essence is contained. The Garden Hose of Unspeakable Evil, for instance, will instantly wither any flowers it waters—probably a good thing, since you're trying to turn everything around you into a barren wasteland, and having a garden hose of this variety can be a time saver.

If you ignore this advice and put your power into a single small object, don't let it out of your sight. Keep it around your neck, on a chain of unbreakable adamant, and surround yourself with a bodyguard of really, really big Orcs that are prepared to die for you in order to prevent anyone from getting within ten feet of the chain. Don't take it off when you go to sleep at night (assuming you sleep). And as soon as possible, transfer some of the power to something else as a backup. Also, change out the personnel in your Orc body-guards every couple of weeks. This can be determined by putting the Orcs in a room with two daggers and waiting to see who comes out alive.

2. **If you own a *palantir* and make mental contact with a small, apparently unimportant hobbit who seems to have wandered into your Stone of Seeing by mistake, don't wait to question him until you get him in your Tower.** Go through his mind now and drain everything out of it. Use a corkscrew, if necessary. Of course, by the time he gets to your Tower, he'll be a drooling, gibbering idiot, but does that really matter? The important thing is to find out what he knows. It could be critical information, or it could be pointless stuff, but already knowing what he knows may make a difference someday.

Information is a valuable commodity to Evil Overlords; don't overlook its importance in maintaining law and order throughout your realm. The more you know, the easier you'll sleep at night (unless, of course, you prefer to work through the night and sleep during the day, which a lot of Evil Over-lords like to do, since it makes them seem creepier). The bet-ter a line you have on your opponent, the more secure you are, and even the smallest and least important enemy may have some valuable information. Best get it out of him now while you have him on the line.

And don't gloat over your little font of information while you're draining his mind. Gloating is a pointless habit that probably gets more Evil Overlords killed than all the brave heroes and adventurers combined can account for. There will be plenty of time for gloating when you're the supreme ruler of the world and are busy covering the lands in a second darkness. Right now you have other things to worry about.

3. **If you're fortunate enough to catch a white wizard, don't waste time trying to turn him to the dark side.** Kill him. Don't imprison him until you can devise a fitting end for him. Just kill him. Above all, as noted above, don't stick him on the roof of your tower where he can be rescued by eagles. He belongs in a dungeon, well below the deepest well, where he will be gnawed by rats until you execute him ... which should be sooner rather than later. Wizards are nothing but mischief, and one less walking around is all to the good.

   As mentioned earlier, white wizards are a bit on the dim side, and they're not really all that difficult to catch. Just tell them that a party of hobbits is in trouble somewhere or that there's some free pipe-weed available at your tower and they go haring about the countryside without any precautions. You can snap them up one by one and eliminate them without muss or fuss.

4. **Just because a race of people is small and hitherto unnoticed and spends most of its time getting drunk and smoking pipe-weed doesn't mean you should ignore it.** If you want to be an Evil Overlord and go the distance, you've got to be interested in everything that goes on in Middle-earth. It's true that there are a lot of unimportant things that go on there. This isn't to suggest, for instance, that you have to pay attention every time there's a power shift in the

ruling houses of the Dwarves; after all, they shift rulers more often than a goblin on its second cup of coffee shifts its ... well, anyway, no need to overdo things. But the point is that there are a lot of hitherto unimportant people in Middle-earth who have suddenly started, through no fault or intention of their own, to become important. And those are the ones you should pay attention to.

In particular, if any of them (a) start to suddenly turn invisible, (b) are able to beat off attacks of massive spiders, or (c) are connected with the killings of dragons, these situations require your scrutiny. Any of these things may indicate they've come across a source of power that doesn't rightfully belong to them. In such cases, employ the following procedures: First, kill all of them. Second, search them *very* carefully. Third, find out if any of them have had any dealings with Elves.

It's always Elves who start the problems. But enough about them. They can be easily crushed if you don't mind crushing things—and Elves are more fun to crush than most others.

5. **It's all very well to keep your soldiery divided and fighting with each other (since that's how you prevent an uprising), but when you do that, make sure they don't lose sight of the big picture and overlook the Key to Your Downfall when it's staring them in their big, ugly faces.** If Peril, small and unnoticed, is creeping into your realm—and it usually is—tell your Orcs to be especially vigilant in guarding the borders and to report anything they find and anyone they stop to you *immediately.* You can soften the order by telling them that if they don't

follow it to the letter, you won't have them boiled in oil—
you'll have them torn into bite-size pieces by stone trolls ...
and then boiled in oil.

6. **Don't trust your Orc generals.** They are, at best, unreliable.
If you want something done right, do it yourself. That's usually the best idea. If you want to besiege a stronghold of Men
with your army of thousands upon thousands of screaming
Orcs, at least make a token appearance on the battlefield to
inspire them. You don't have to actually fight. Just be there
and appear to command the troops. You can stay far back
enough to avoid being hit with a stray arrow.

7. **Don't piss off ancient nature spirits or guardians.** These
things are touchy enough without going out of your way to
get them mad at you. Just when you think you've got everything nicely wrapped up, along comes a big honking bunch
of trees and everything goes to pieces. You can probably
pay off these creatures in some fashion. Offer them bushes
or something.

8. **Don't rely too heavily on enspelled allies.** Even though
you may have subverted the local royalty so that it isn't actively hostile to you and may actually hinder your opponents,
don't base your whole strategy on that. There's always some
blundering old idiot of a white wizard who comes along at the
last minute and breaks your spell. Look on this sort of thing
as a delaying tactic, not a strategic centerpiece.

9. **If you do have someone enspelled, and his kingdom has
a lot of really fast horses, don't hesitate to kill them.**
Horses can move fast, and highly trained horsemen move
even faster. Speed is often the name of the game. There's

no point in giving the enemy the advantage of speed. He'll take it, believe me!

10. **If you're going to have an evil henchman, don't constantly insult him, slap him, and kick him in the face.** Let's face it, everyone likes to torture a minion, but there's no reason to damage him unnecessarily. Besides, it makes him so angry. If you're not careful, he might cut your throat.

It's a Troll's Life

Lessons in Self-Preservation From the
Habits and Behaviors of Trolls

Three very large persons sitting round a very large fire of beech logs ... but they were trolls. Obviously trolls. Even Bilbo, in spite of his sheltered life, could see that: from the great heavy faces of them, and their size, and the shape of their legs, not to mention their language, which was not drawing-room fashion at all, at all.

—From J.R.R. Tolkien's *The Hobbit*

Trolls work as little as possible. They play dirty and have voracious appetites. They keep company with those who share their interests, can be exploited, or can be taken advantage of or benefitted from. While groups of trolls may work together, every individual troll is out for himself in the end.

Well, aren't we all?

Trolls may form raiding parties or groups in which they travel. They may forage, steal, hunt, and dine together—but none of this is likely to occur without a fight. The fight may be over anything from their allotted portion of the spoils to divisions of labor to what's for dinner. But one thing is certain: Trolls will be trolls, and sooner or later they'll fight about something.

TYPES OF TROLLS

While a troll is basically a troll and the very name is pretty much a definition of the creature itself, a few varieties of trolls do exist.

Their differences—which are dictated mainly by habitat and living conditions—aren't too great, but they are worth noting.

- **Stone Trolls:** These common trolls are unfairly named for an unfortunate weakness that most trolls suffer. In fact, unless a troll is specific to one of the varieties mentioned below, it very well could be called a stone troll. All trolls (with the exception of the Olog-hai) turn to stone when exposed to daylight unless the Dark Lord Sauron has put them under a protective spell. Because of this, trolls are for the most part nocturnal creatures. Any daytime dealings of trolls typically occur in caves that block the light of the sun.

- **Hill Trolls:** These trolls are named for the hilly regions where they typically reside in the Ettenmoors or Angmar. They are said to sometimes migrate to the Trollshaws during winter. They are known to dig small caves into hill faces. For some unknown reason, hill trolls seem to be more concerned with clothing than other trolls. They often wear a crude set of brown leather overalls.

- **Cave Trolls:** A race of trolls that live in the caves of the Misty Mountains. Larger and less intelligent than hill trolls, cave trolls have thick hides that will easily notch a sword. They have poor eyesight and rely on their sense of smell. They are clumsy and brutish and will kill and eat pretty much anything that comes within arm's reach.

- **Mountain Trolls:** This largest species of troll is found in the mountains of Middle-earth. They are smarter than cave trolls. These creatures are very strong and are able to lift massive boulders (and other objects) and hurl them as makeshift weapons, which makes them quite formidable in battle.

- **Snow Trolls:** These trolls live in the northern frozen wastelands of Angmar, the home of the Witch-king leader of the Nazgûl. They are typically shorter than other troll species and have a white or light gray fur that allows them to blend in with their snow-covered surroundings.

- **Two-Headed Trolls:** These trolls—obviously named for having two heads—are rare and hardly ever seen but may well exist. Some believe they live hidden away in the Ettenmoors. In fact, that priggish wizard Gandalf made reference to them, saying, "I'm afraid trolls do behave like that, even those with one head each."

- **Olog-hai:** A breed of fierce and intelligent trolls created specifically for battle by the Dark Lord Sauron, not unlike the Uruk-hai (which were derived from Orcs). These trolls are much larger, stronger, and smarter, and are impervious to sunlight. An Olog-hai is the ultimate fighting troll.

Why Do Trolls Turn to Stone?

Trolls were created by a spell of the spirit Morgoth (also known as Melkor) in a time of darkness (before the age of the sun). They were created in mockery of the living tree-creatures known as the Ents. Being trees, the Ents were made of wood, and so the trolls were created from stone. Because trolls were made in darkness, when the light falls upon them the spell is broken, which causes their stonelike armored body tissue to fully petrify.

HABITATS & DWELLINGS

Much of what makes a troll a troll has to do with its surroundings. That's why different troll species are often named after the areas in which they reside (for example, mountain trolls make their homes in the sides of mountains and cave trolls live in caverns). Because they are so lazy and uninventive, a troll's lifestyle is dictated by its environment. They aren't very particular about much of anything and will use whatever tools are readily available to them (such as rocks for smashing things that are in their way... you know, like other rocks).

As previously mentioned, most trolls live in darkness by necessity. It is also interesting that despite their large stature, most trolls prefer close quarters—they prefer the earthen walls and ceilings of caves, caverns, and crevices. A troll doesn't have much use for anything other than what is nearby and has no real interest in open spaces.

TROLL BEHAVIOR & CONDUCT

Despite being brutish and not incredibly bright, you can learn a lot about self-preservation from a troll. Here are a few examples.

- Trolls tend to be very self-centered. They are motivated by food, drink, wealth, and not much else. But hey, if you don't look after yourself, then who will? Follow the food, the drink, and the money, and you'll have a better chance of landing on your feet.

- Most trolls fear the sunlight for obvious reasons. Even the Olog-hai, whom Sauron crossbred to have no such weakness, would prefer to live in caves and avoid the light whenever possible. While you probably don't have to worry about turning into stone from sun exposure (unless you are, in fact, a troll—which is unlikely since most trolls don't read), it is a good idea to avoid your own weaknesses.

- Most troll races, while not very intelligent, do have a basic understanding of language. They aren't typically great conversationalists, but while in the company of other trolls they may strive to insult and curse each other well. One has to take pride in something, and expressing yourself with some well-placed profanity is as worthwhile a pursuit as any.

- Trolls are lazy. They strive to gain as much as possible while doing as little as possible. By following their example, you'll likely stay out of trouble. No problem with hanging back and letting someone else do the heavy lifting. It will save your back—and other parts, too.

- Trolls have few morals. Killing, stealing, and taking whatever is within reach are all common behaviors—especially when the object of interest is easy pickings. Don't let morals get in the way of what you want. Silly morals, they'll only get you into trouble—"burning alive in the fires of Mount Doom" kind of trouble.

- Camaraderie among trolls is rare but not unheard of. Trolls will band together when it is mutually beneficial, though fellowships between trolls rarely last very long. How can they, when you're constantly considering who amongst your group of peers you can exploit, who has just enough to offer without posing a threat, or which troll you want to recruit for whatever dark deed you have in mind?

While trolls are brutish and not very bright, they tend to thrive. They have very basic needs and live fairly simply. This simplicity serves them well. Follow their example and you are more likely to lead a longer life—albeit not a very glamorous one.

DINING LIKE A TROLL

Like hobbits, trolls are largely motivated by food—though the food doesn't tend to be as well prepared or tasty as hobbit food. Trolls like to eat a lot and often, and they don't care too much about what they're eating—as long as it's meat. They like mutton, chicken, squab, venison, coney, hobbit, Dwarf … all kinds of meat. And they love to wash it all down with lots and lots of ale.

The Eating Habits of Trolls

Trolls don't have a set etiquette that they follow for dining. But you'll notice a few tendencies that make sense when you consider the company they keep. Troll-like manners may serve you well when you dine with your villainous cohorts.

- Trolls usually eat with their hands, partly because they are uncouth but also because trolls don't trust one another. Utensils may be used as weapons. A troll wouldn't think twice about driving the tongs of a fork into another troll's eye over something as simple as the last dinner roll.

- When dining together, the general rule of eating among trolls is that if you snooze, you lose. Grab the food fast to make sure you get the biggest and best parts. Gobble everything down quickly and go back for seconds, thirds, and fourths.

- Eat until you can't eat anymore—you never know when you'll eat next.

- Travel on your stomach. Let your appetite play a large role in the way you travel and the places you go, and you'll be much less likely to go hungry.

Trolls as Cooks

Trolls are not the best cooks in Middle-earth, but they aren't necessarily the worst cooks, either. As it has been said, trolls love to eat, and they think about food a great deal. Their methods of cooking are usually rather simple. They often boil their food or roast it over an open fire. They also like to tenderize their meat by smacking it with a mallet or sometimes a nice flat rock. Trolls are also fond of gravy and tend to top anything they prepare with the thick stuff. So if you like simply seasoned roasted meat and soups, or stews that are largely comprised of meat and potatoes, you'll find that troll food isn't all that bad. And trolls love ale, so you'll likely find a decent barrel of something to drink wherever a troll-prepared dinner is to be had. Chase any food with enough ale, and I'll wager you'll find it palatable enough.

Typical Troll Preparation for Roasted Mutton With Gravy

1. Catch an adult sheep and field dress it with a knife, axe, or sharp rock. Remove the skin, head, and viscera (save the heart, liver, and lungs for stew, if you want).

2. Create a seasoning made from a couple of handfuls each of coarse salt, pepper, and any herbs you can find (rosemary, mint, sage, thyme, and coriander will all work). Rub the meat with the seasoning.

3. Use the branch of a young tree to create a spit, and hang the sheep over a fire that has died down by half. The mutton should roast for several hours. As the mutton roasts, catch the juices and drippings from the meat in a pot or saucepan.

4. Find a spot at the edge of the fire for your pot of drippings, add some flour, salt, and pepper, and stir until you have gravy. Thicken with more flour and season to taste.

5. Serve hot from the fire with beer or ale and a stale loaf of stolen bread and cheese, if you have it.

STRENGTH IN NUMBERS

Trolls don't care too much for company. They don't like anyone or anything very much aside from food, beer, and treasure. So when trolls ban together, you can bet there's a reason. And the reason usually involves—you guessed it—food, beer, or treasure.

On a very base level, trolls know the value of working together and will form temporary groups or raiding parties. They put aside their troll-ish differences and set out to achieve their mutual goal without much thought to how they will divide the spoils of their endeavor. As you can imagine, arguments break out soon after the deed is done. Usually the matter of "who gets what and how much" is settled through a physical brawl that involves all parties. The one left standing takes everything.

FIGHTING LIKE A TROLL

When it comes to hand-to-hand combat, trolls fare quite well. Less effective methods of battle certainly exist. Trolls rely on smashing, squashing, clobbering, walloping, and chomping their enemies. There's absolutely no artistry or honor in the way trolls fight, but don't let a lack of technique fool you into thinking troll-style combat isn't powerful or effective. Many an Orc or goblin army has gone into battle with a "pet" troll in their ranks. And when some extra brute strength is called for, they let the beast off the leash. Of course, not everyone can fight like a troll—the small and the puny may be better off resorting to strategy, subterfuge, diversion, deception, and trickery. But "smash and bash" works well as a battle strategy if you have the muscle mass to back up your plan (or lack of one, rather). So if you're a fellow bruiser, read on.

Hand to Hand

As has been pointed out, there's nothing fancy about troll combat. Strikes are generally rough punches or clubbing motions executed with the fist. Open palm slaps are sometimes used for general wallops or to squash a smaller enemy. The employment of kicks in troll combat is rather rare, though trolls are known to stomp on a fallen enemy. These kinds of strikes can be slow to land (unlike a quick jab or swift kick) but generally have a lot of power, and they can do plenty of damage if the opponent is caught off guard.

The Perfect Troll-Style Palm Slap

Executing a good openhanded slap is all about momentum. Straighten your arm and loosely swing it behind you before slinging it in a wide arc toward your opponent. Keep your palm open while performing this motion. Land your strike on the side of your opponent's head. Aim for the cheek to cause minimal damage (this sort of strike is good for a spat over the last piece of bacon with some fellows you generally like well enough). If you want to do more damage, cup your hand slightly and aim for your opponent's ear. This can be a devastating blow when landed correctly, as your cupped hand can force air into the ear canal and cause a good deal of pain and disorientation—possibly even a concussion.

The Backhand

Another good troll-like move is a nice solid backhand. This technique is for all intents and purposes the opposite of the open-palm slap previously described. Begin the backhand by raising your hand to your opposite shoulder. Then loosely straighten your arm and swing it in a wide motion toward your opponent's head. You can either keep an open hand and slap your opponent with the back of your hand, or you can close your fist and hit him with your knuckles like a club. A good strategy is to use an open hand if you are aiming for the eyes and a closed fist if aiming for the nose or the temple (any of these targets can be devastated by such a blow).

The Hammer Fist

When facing an opponent shorter than yourself (particular someone with a scrawny neck), a great tactic is the hammer fist. Simply swing your tightly clenched fist high in the air and bring it down firmly on the top of your enemy's head, as if you were driving a nail into a piece of wood. Repeat as necessary.

The Stomp Kick

Trolls don't put a lot of thought into any of their strikes—these techniques come pretty naturally for anyone, to tell the truth. You can maximize their effectiveness, however, simply by studying the mechanics of each motion. Stomping on something, for example, doesn't seem like it requires much thought—and it doesn't. But if you break it down and make sure you raise your knee as high as you can and lead with the heel of your foot when you land the stomp, the technique will be much more effective. There is a tendency to simply stomp using the flat of the foot, which won't inflict nearly as much pain (assuming that pain is your goal).

Weapons

Trolls weapons, much like the trolls themselves, are usually blunt instruments. Trolls tend to favor such weapons as cudgels, clubs, maces, mallets, and war-hammers and enjoy pounding their enemies into a mushy red paste.

- **Cudgels and clubs:** These are the simplest of all weapons. A cudgel or club is nothing more than a short stick (usually made of a very hard, dense variety of wood). They are usually wielded with one hand, though at times a two-handed attack may be employed (particularly if the cudgel is a larger one).

- **Maces:** A mace is basically a more sophisticated cudgel. It has the addition of spikes or knobs at the end, which enhances the damage that the instrument is capable of delivering. A mace may be forged of metal rather than wood; however such a tool is pretty fancy for a troll, and any troll wielding one has likely been conscripted into the service of the Dark Lord.

- **Mallets:** A mallet is a kind of hammer that is made of wood and typically has a large, broad head. Trolls use these simple tools for a number of purposes, from food preparation to the crude construction of simple shelters. And, of course, they are also great for smacking an opponent on the head.

- **War-hammers:** A war-hammer is a large hammer forged of metal and created for the express purpose of use in battle. War-hammers can vary in construction, from short-handled hammers for close-quarters combat to long-handled hammers (also known as mauls), which can be used effectively against mounted riders. A war-hammer may also be adapted with any number of spikes upon its surface (one at the top or one instead of a double hammer face or one at the bottom of the handle—there are all kinds of wicked variations).

A TROLL JUST IS

Trolls are not great thinkers. They don't mull things over or ask questions or contemplate the whys and wherefores of life. They exist to exist. They plod along unhappily in their daily lives, smashing and bashing whatever gets in their way. They have no real aspiration or purpose—unless of course they are being directed by Sauron on some mission of heavy destruction or are being led into glorious battle by an army of Orcs. A troll's life is a simple existence, really. Trolls are angry and evil, to be sure. But they are happy being angry and evil. And there's something kind of Zen about that.

Orcs and the Art of Warmongering

Classic Philosophy of Warfare as Retold by the Uruk-hai

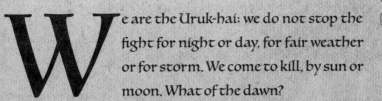

We are the Uruk-hai: we do not stop the fight for night or day, for fair weather or for storm. We come to kill, by sun or moon. What of the dawn?

—From J.R.R. Tolkien's *The Two Towers*

Every civilization has its great armies, and its leaders often keep notes, writings, and poems about their fighting strategies and military philosophies. One example is *The Art of War* by Sun Tzu, a text of the age of Men that has been revered by generals, strategists, and heads of business for centuries.

In the days of old, before the reign of Men, great armies were not always human. One of the greatest armies of all was the fighting Uruk-hai, a race of Orcs created first by Sauron and then further mutated by the wizard Saruman. These Orcs were larger, smarter, fiercer, and more capable than typical Orcs, and they marched across Middle-earth raining down all manner of destruction.

The Uruk-hai were not military scholars in the same way that many generals throughout the ages have been. But there is something indeed to be learned from their cruel methods and merciless tactics. If the Uruk-hai had written a text such as *The Art of War*, what might it look like? How might it shape the art of fighting? What forces might use it today? Journey into the mind of a fighting Orc and see what cruel ideas might inspire you in battle.

What follows is an imagining of a treatise on warfare as it might have been written by the Orcs.

STRATEGY

Military action is important to the Land of Mordor—
the field of battle is death and life, the will of Sauron
is power and destruction, so it is imperative to study it.

The power and supremacy of the Dark Lord Sauron
depends upon military action, so it is necessary
to study it carefully.

Location is paramount in war.
The high ground is the ground of victory—
the low ground means death.

Success or death, victory or defeat depends
on the configuration of the field of battle
and on the way of the battle.

Assess the campaign in terms of five conditions:
the way, the weather, the ground, the commander, the troops.

The way means the military force should have the same goal
as the Dark Lord Sauron, so that they will share death or share
success without fear.

The weather and the seasons must be considered.
Military action at an unfavorable time may bring
about defeat and demise.

The ground means the terrain and the field of battle.
It must be assessed for travel, provisions, and strategic positions.

The commander must enforce the will of the Dark Lord.
And impress upon the troops His will.
The commander is the instrument of the Dark Lord.

The troops must follow the commander.
The troops must bow to the will of the Dark Lord.
Those who do not are doomed to die.

The rules of the commander shall not be broken.
They are the rules of the Dark Lord.
Any offenders will be punished.

Under the eye of Sauron all are equal.
Under the eye of Sauron all will serve.
Under the eye of Sauron all will be awarded what they deserve.

When a reward is deserved, it shall be given.
When a punishment is deserved, it shall be given.

By assessing and ensuring these things, you can prevail
in the name of Sauron.
If you do not prevail, you have failed
in the name of Sauron.
And you will receive punishment.

When attacking an enemy,
it is best to attack when they are unprepared.
When they expect it, it is best to wait.
When they are lazy and content, then attack.

Lure your enemy with promise of victory.
Then, in the confusion of battle, destroy them.

Cause them to doubt one another.
Bribe a weak individual with promise of power
or amnesty under the eye of Sauron.
Send him into their ranks and let the corruption
destroy them from within.

Take away the energy of your enemy's army.
Take away the heart of their generals.

Cause division amongst their leadership and their ranks.
Then launch your attack.

Win the battle before you step onto the battlefield.
Know that you will succeed in the name of the Dark Lord.
Or else you shall surely die.

BATTLE

Even when you are winning in battle,
you must take care not to exhaust your strength.
If the day is meant to be long,
see to your troops and your supplies.
Send for reinforcements.

When your forces are tired and hungry
and your weapons are dulled,
be at your most wary.
Your enemy will surely rise up
at the worst of times.

Your strike should be swift and merciless.
It is never good for a battle to wage for very long.
The day must be won for the Dark Lord quickly and efficiently.

The longer the battle,
the greater the possibility of defeat.
And defeat means punishment in the fires of Mount Doom.

When your captains are overconfident,
when your troops are content and lazy,
when stomachs are too full,
you are at your greatest disadvantage.

Feed your troops before journeying to the battleground;
after that, let them feed on the enemy's scattered entrails.

Troops should be strong,
but they should also be hungry.
In this way, they will be as sharp
as the sharpest sword.

Travel light.
Carry arms from Mordor,
but find supplies on the battlefield,
and feast upon the spoils of war.

Conscript locals into your service.
Give them wooden shields
and send them into battle before you.
In this way you'll conserve your warriors.

Control the food and control the battle.
Take the enemy's resources for your own
or ruin them.

Reward your troops with spoils of war.
They will fight harder in hopes of
winning the enemy's food stores.

Destroy your enemy utterly,
or conscript them into the Dark Lord's service.

Overcome your enemy
and increase the strength and reach of the Dark Lord.

SIEGE

If you cannot bend a nation's will to that of the Dark Lord's,
then you must utterly destroy it and its people.

Penetrate your enemy's territory.
Block their stronghold from the world outside.
Cut off all communications.
Force them to surrender,
or die.

Victory is the important thing.
Killing is good, too.
Use strategy and the influence of the Dark Lord
to achieve one or the other.

Rendering another army helpless and forcing surrender
without killing all the solders is admirable
if you can conscript them into the service of the Dark Lord.
Otherwise, kill them all.

When you do battle, it is necessary to kill.
It is also fun.

Strike such fear in the hearts of your enemies
that they will come to surrender immediately.
Then kill a few for good measure
to put them in their place.

Strike early, while your enemy
is still making plans.
Talking is for the weak.
Let swift and devastating action speak for you.

Attack allies and neighbors of your enemy
as soon as you learn of them.
Destroy all allegiances
other than those to the Dark Lord.

Attack their cities and burn their towns.
This will devastate them,
and they will have no choice
but to bow before the Dark Lord.

In a siege there will be casualties.
Make sure to use devastating force
and keep the casualties on their side—
not yours.

Ruin their plans.
Spoil their fellowships.

Cut off their provisions.
And they will surrender.

If you outnumber your enemy,
surround them.
If you are equal in number,
stand and fight.
If you are lesser in number,
lay down your life in the name of Sauron, if necessary.

FORMATION & FORCE

First make yourself invincible,
then find your enemy's weakness.

Keep order in the ranks.
Watch for troops in your command
who aren't pulling their weight.
Summarily deal with those who shirk their duties.

You cannot force your enemy to make mistakes;
you must be vigilant
and take advantage of their mistakes
when they happen.

Victory in battle is achieved
by positioning yourself
where you will certainly win.

Gain ground and you will win.
Lose ground and you will be defeated.

Go into battle
like a flood into a valley,
like the wind howls through a mountain pass,
like a thunderstorm spreads across the land.

Seek victory in battle
through the force of momentum.
Descend upon your enemy
like rocks rolling down a mountain.

PUSH & PULL

Good warriors cause their enemy to come to them.
Lure them with the prospect of victory,
then strike them down in the name of the Dark Lord.

Attack suddenly.
Burn their supplies.
Raze their fields.
Cut off communications.
And they will run.

Cut them off.
There is no rescue.
There is no escape.

There is only surrender,
or death.

A successful attack—
your enemy won't know where to defend.
A successful defense—
your enemy won't know where to attack.

Whether your enemy
lives or dies
depends on you.
You are the master
of your enemy's fate.

When you want to fight an enemy,
attack what he will surely defend.

Be unpredictable like fire.
Be immovable as a mountain.

Your force should have no constant formation.
Change shape and adapt
according to your enemy.
This is the path to victory
in the name of the Dark Lord.

Urkl's Guide to What the Well-Dressed Villian Is Wearing These Days

rkl here, recently appointed Chief Armorer and Sartorial Adviser to His Most Sacred Awfulness the Lord of the Orcs of the Misty Mountains. (I know, I know, that title is so *embarrassing*. Such a mouthful. But what can I say? They *love* me up there.) Now, I know what you're all thinking: *What* was I trying to say with that iron armor at the Battle of Five Armies? After all, it didn't do me much good when that awful bear-man was crushing the life out of me, did it? So why didn't I go for something more, well, *massive*? Well, darlings, to get right to the point, sometimes the fashion statement is much more important than winning some silly battle, if you know what I mean. I know all the other Orcs were wearing horrible, cobbled-together leather armor with bits of steel sewn on in odd places, but I wouldn't be caught dead in a get-up like that.

Honestly, sometimes the fashion choices made by our side in the Great War are just too, too awful. If you're going to be a Dark Lord, intent of bringing all the world under your shadow, well, you have to look the part, don't you? And no one on our side seems to have the faintest idea of how to wear intimidating clothing. What's with all that slouching and slumping the Orc armies do? Orcs are supposed to be the bringers of the future, the first wave of a brave new world dominated by the Dark Lord. You can't demonstrate that sort of resolve by slumping. It *ruins* the line of the clothes.

Really, it's enough to make one cry in frustration.

So that's why I've decided to put down in plain black and white (with just a smidgen of red and a bit of taupe around the edges of the pages) exactly what everyone who is anyone should be wearing this season. After that, I'll send it off to Him in Dol Gulder, or whatever horrible place He's settled in now. And he can redesign everyone's uniforms—and I don't need to tell you that they're *screaming* for makeovers.

Well, then. Where to start? Let's begin with Orcs.

ORCS

Now, I'd be the *last* person to say that Orcs are going to win any awards in the bodily cleanliness department, but at least they should *look* as if they're battle ready. An Orc preparing to go into a fight (is there any other kind of Orc?) should be dressed in the latest in fashionable fight wear. This means boiled leather armor at its foundation (and you can always steam away those pesky bloodstains in the vent of a volcano) covered with strips of metal to guard against flying arrows or sword blows. The legs have high leather boots, although many Orcs don't wear boots since they hurt their feet. For the head we have a *darling* helmet with a big pointy snout made of metal and two holes, one on either side of the head, to let the ears out. There's a bit of chain mail hanging down at the back of the helmet to cover the neck and prevent one's head from being cut off, since having one's head cut off *does* slow one down in battle.

People ask me all the time, "Urkl, but what about sigils? Even *you* can't make evil sigils attractive!" Well, chickadees, just watch.

We start with the basic red eye, of course, because that's what He decreed all His armies would carry, and we know His word is law around here. But we can elaborate a bit on that, can't we? Who's to stop us from making some wee little *improvements*? What about some nice, long, fluttery lashes around the eye? And instead of all red, let's just add a bit of yellow around the rim so it becomes flamelike. So. We can also draw a bit of eyeliner above and below, to make it stand out, and add just a smidgen of orange eye shadow. So. Now just a light wash of silver where the eyelid would be, and there you have it! An eye any soldier would be proud to carry on his shield—that is, if he's not carrying around real eyes.

Of course, if you don't want to sport the eye, an alternative is to bring along the White Hand. That offers a little more room for creativity, munchkins. I mean, we can just go to town with that, can't we?

Well, *no*, we can't. I was being sarcastic. Could you tell? Honestly, a *white hand*? What could be more boring? Now, I say if you want a scary symbol or something, why not put the hand in a ring? I mean, what are we fighting about, anyway? Make the ring glow with a sort of deadly fire—*mithril* would be perfect, but it's *so* hard to get hold of these days; I don't know what everyone is using it for—and outline the hand in a little red (perhaps paint the fingernails with red blood drops … Ooooooo! Creepy!). You can put it on your Orc's armor or his shield, right in the center or just a *leetle* off to one side and up to make the balance seem better.

I don't know about you, possums, but I insist on only the best sewing on my Orcs' leather armor. Absolutely! A dozen stitches to the inch or I give the armorers a beating. Well, *I* don't, of course, but I have Orcs who do that sort of thing for me.

Speaking of shields, darlings, your Orc-in-battle doesn't want something gauche and heavy dragging him down. Instead, he wants something that will really accessorize his whole outfit. The rule here? The length from the top to the bottom of the shield should never be more than the distance from the middle of the shoulder to the very tippy tips of the fingers when the arm is outstretched. That's so much more pleasing than those *horrible* things everyone used to drag into fights. And a smaller shield means it's easier to move around, block arrows, smash your opponent in the face, and so on.

Well, what about swords, you ask. Well, what about them? After all, a sword isn't just a weapon; it *completes* an outfit and really takes it to the next level. That's what I always say. So sword selection is really important. After all, you want what you're wearing to make a statement.

Fashion these days dictates curved swords. I'm going to go all contrary here and say that curved swords (or "scimitars," as some people call them) are just a passing fad that will quickly fade. You can call me crazy or a bluff old traditionalist, but I say there's nothing like a strong, straight, hard sword for really emphasizing an Orc's ... er ... Orc-hood. Something he can hold erect and really penetrate with and thrust hard into ... Sorry. Had to stop for a little bit. I was getting overexcited.

Right, well, back to swords, darlings. You want a sword that is no longer than the distance from your elbow to your foot when you're standing straight, arms at your sides. Get a friend to help you measure. The sword should be light enough to swing easily and should be stored in a scabbard across your back. The optimum material for a scabbard is leather, which gives the weapon that lovely new sword smell when you draw it.

WOLF RIDERS

Of course, given my inimitable good taste and connections, I've been asked (I can't tell you by whom, but let's just say that his name begins with an *S*, ends with an *N*, and has an *M* somewhere in the middle!) to advise on the proper wear for wolf-riding Orcs. Well! I can tell you I was absolutely *thrilled* when the invitation came. I've given this some very hard thought and was so flushed I had to take a bath and add extra bubbles and scent to the water.

Wolf riders, of course, are the elite shock troops of an Orc army. They ride in front to destroy the enemy outriders and smash up the defenses before the ranks of the infantry get there. Their chief worry when going on the attack is archers. Armor stops arrows, of course, but if the armor's too heavy, it also slows the wolf riders down, when in fact their best weapon is speed.

With that in mind, I've come up with the most cunning chain mail design. It drapes over the front of the rider while leaving his back exposed (any wolf rider going away from the enemy deserves to be shot in the back!). The chain mail is a bright puce with red streamers flying from the upper arms, thighs, and the tip top of the helm. (I wanted to add mauve ribbons onto the ears of the wolves but was told that the Wargs wouldn't allow themselves to be decorated in that way. Philistines!) Each rider carries his shield in front of him and can duck down behind it to avoid arrows, though the chain mail should do a good job of blocking most of them. We did a test charge not that long ago, and between you and me, I don't think anyone has ever seen anything like it. It looked as if a fire was sweeping across the plain.

Dressing the Wargs in anything has proven impossible, so they'll have to stay the way they are. It's a pity, because you've no idea how cunning they'd look with their fur done up in tight curls. Well, I can dream, I suppose.

I see that I mentioned bubble bath and scent, and that reminds me that you really need to know the best way of getting bloodstains out of armor. Lemon juice is the secret, although Elf blood takes quite a lot. Scrub hard, possums, and don't be afraid of the soap. It's not fatal!

TROLLS

Now, trolls. The poor dears—they never get any respect from anyone. I think it's because everyone assumes that if you're a troll you must be stupid, but I've met some very charming trolls. There was a lovely one a few years ago: We sat around talking until the poor thing turned to stone in the morning sun. I was *so* taken aback, I assure you. I didn't eat for two days, I was that upset.

With trolls, we're talking plus sizes. I know that's somewhere no one wants to go, but there's just no two ways about it. I'm rather partial to that sort of thing, myself: Lots of nice rolls of flesh to hold on to and everything. And just because they're a bit on the heavy side, I don't see why trolls should be shortchanged in the manner of battle wear. Up until now, my predecessors dressed them in modified diapers. I mean, *how* déclassé! Yes, their skin is tough as stone, but that doesn't mean everyone wants to see it all the time, warts and all! And do you think trolls don't want to look their best? When they're squishing some nasty Dwarf to a jelly, the last thing they want is to get blood all over themselves. Well, possibly they don't mind, but I certainly do. (Remember what I just said about washing out bloodstains, by the way. Lemon juice does the trick!)

Now, if you think for a minute that I'm going to let trolls go out without something to wear on their heads, well, you're just a big old silly. Trolls *want* helmets. They don't need them, because their skulls are so thick, poor darlings, but that doesn't mean they don't want something that looks really dashing and up to date. So I've designed the most cunning little (big, actually) helms with a golden eye rimmed with silver fire and two of the cutest little eagle feathers at each side. Makes them look as if they're wearing wings. The

Ones in Charge made me take off the feathers; I don't know why. Maybe there was a shortage of eagles.

BALROGS

Well, believe me, I thought about Balrogs. I mean, no one's ever tried to dress one, right? So what kind of a feather in my cap would it be to create some armor for a Balrog to wear into battle?

But then I thought, "Wait a minute! Balrogs are spirits of the underworld. They don't just need battle armor. They need everyday wear, too." I mean, it's not as if they're spending all their time hanging around in the deep, dark places of the world, waiting for a fight to break out. There's the day-to-day routine. They've got to spend their days doing a thousand little errands: picking up the young Balrogs from Corrupted Maia school, doing the weekly shopping, keeping the Mines of Moria clean and tidy. So we need something that's functional and practical. Something that's strong, washable, and above all, fire resistant. I puzzled over this for weeks, I can tell you.

Then it came to me.

Weavable rock.

Well, I mean, if they can make a mail shirt or two out of *mithril*, I said to myself, surely I can whip up something from rock that can be woven and sewn. (And, as it turns out, I did have to whip up my research and development team a bit, the slackers. But it's all right. They're almost all recovering and should be back on the job as soon as their backs and legs heal. As for those who won't be returning, well, I needed a bit of fresh blood on that team anyway. And believe me when I say their blood is *fresh*!)

Yes, weavable rock is clearly the answer to the everyday needs of your average Balrog. At the end of the day, just dip it in a pit of molten lava, leave it to dry overnight, and in the morning you're good to go. No fuss, no muss. Stops all arrows, axes, swords (even most magical ones, too), and it can even withstand a direct hit from a wizard's staff. So my research assistants assure me.

Of course, there's nothing like a practical test, so I sent a small party with a shirt I'd created to Moria to have a chat with the Balrog who lives there. I haven't heard back from them, now that I think of it, and it's been more than six months. I wonder what's keeping them.

I did have my research Orcs try it out. It took four or five of them to even hold the thing up. But after we'd shot arrows at it and hacked at it for a while with axes, I can report that it lives up to *all* its promise. I'm so excited about this, I've got to sit down for a minute.

There. I'm back.

NAZGÛL

I know, I know, I can just imagine what you're saying, dears. Nazgûl don't *need* any protection, because they have *magic*. You can't even kill the head one if you're merely a Man. So why do they need to worry about the winds of fashion?

It's perfectly simple. They're the apple of His Eye (literally His *Eye*!) and he wants them to look their best. You can't have them flying about Middle-earth spreading terror, death, and destruction (not to mention wailing on the occasional party of hobbits) without looking their best. And best, here, means creepy, weird, and sexy. Yes, I said sexy. It's the way to go for the well-dressed Nazgûl.

Now, mind you, I'm not suggesting for a minute that we talk about see-through black robes and hip-high slits up the side—although that would *certainly* be interesting and I wouldn't like to exclude it for future epics. But let's all remember that black is the new ... black. What we need in the way of black robes is not your ordinary black, rumpled, dusty, weatherworn robes your father witch-king wore. You need ... black velvet.

Yes, I know you're shocked. Urkl is going traditional, possums. But consider: Black velvet is opulent yet wearable, adapts well to all kinds of weather, and we don't need to worry about the horrible fake ruching effect you get with silk or crinoline or some of those other fabrics. Velvet sort of just ... *falls* around the nonexistent body inside the robe. I mean it follows the body line *so well*. But it billows out at the appropriate times ... and the way it seems to *absorb* the light! Well! Nothing could be better for an encounter at the summit of Weathertop.

Now, of course, velvet tends not to wear well, and it gets ruffled up in the wrong direction by all sorts of things, like a mean old Ranger's magic sword (well, half sword, really. Is that a comment on the fact that he could never get it up? Oooooh! I can't believe I just said that.)

Well, possums, what I say is that where sewing and fashion fails, magic always finds a way. I'm sure that as soon as the Nazgûl see the wonderful black velvet robes I've designed for them, they'll be as pleased as, oh, it's possible for undead spirits to be pleased. Why, they'll be a black velvet band.

NAZGÛL BEASTS

No, we're not going to leave out the beasts that the Nazgûl ride on. Just because they're bloodsucking, bone-crunching, soul-destroying creatures from the pits of Morgoth himself doesn't mean they shouldn't look their best.

Now, my feeling has always been that when equipping animals (or things that sort of look like animals, anyway) we should try to focus on the animal's chief function. In the Nazgûl beast's case, it's to kill everything that comes near it, so some sort of flexible armor to stop the odd arrow or slashing cut of a sword wielded by a blonde *woman* is probably indicated. A kind of neck collar, for instance, to prevent its neck from being slashed off in a single blow. So that's what I designed: a large, thick neck collar. Would you believe that the nasty thing simply rejected it out of hand?

I told it to its face ... or what passes for a face on it, "You'll be very sorry one of these days when a blonde-haired female pretending to be a man cuts off your head. You'll be very sorry. You'll think, 'I'd be glad of that big neck collar that Urkl offered me. I'd be very glad of it right now when my head is being cut off.'" That's what I said to it.

Well, I thought about saying it, but it was very big and drooling a lot, with the leg of an Orc sticking out of its mouth. So I *thought* about saying it. And I probably *would* have said it if its master hadn't come by and asked what I wanted. And, do you know, I didn't have a *thing* to say to him.

DARK LORDS

Now, I know you've been saying to yourselves. "But Urkl! What about the dark lords? We can't leave them out, can we?"

Well, of course not! Not for a moment. Get that idea right out of your silly head. With dark lords, we have to remember that the name of the game is mystery. Secrecy. The mysterious, legendary figure whose name appears as the dark ending of stories that are told round the fire to frightened children.

Brrrr! I'm quite chilled myself.

And ordinary clothes just won't do. They 're okay for subordinates and for creatures who worship Him. But He just doesn't want to be the same as anyone else. Believe me, I know. I have spent *days* on this problem. Really.

Now, for a start, remember that there's only one Him. That's very important, and if you don't remember, He'll remind you. So let's start with the lesser dark lords, the ones who are just ordinarily scary.

Well, I think what really works for scary is something that's just a *bit* on the crinkly-crunchy side, so I'm suggesting crinoline for the robes. I know, I know. It's going in a very radical direction, and I'm usually such an old traditionalist. But think about it. What could be more upsetting to His enemies than realizing that he's on the very *cutting edge* of fashion? And crinoline really just *works* for him. The only problem is that it isn't flame retardant, so I'm still working on that. After all, even though it's *very* impressive when his robes burst into flames every time he enters a room, there's the budget to be considered. He spoke to me about this the last time we talked—and we talk *often*, indeed we do, poopsies, because I'm His *favorite* designer. Indeed, he's given me permission to design the new livery for the servants of the Black Tower, and that's a design challenge, I can tell you.

First of all, there are a *lot* of servants. He believes in changing out servants every few days, and I can't just use the same robes for all of them; I mean, bloodstains, even with lemon juice, are a *pain* to get out. And *who* has that kind of time? So I said to myself, I said, "Urkl, what do great people really want? They don't want to be bothered with details." And so I sat down at my drawing board and created something quite special for Him.

Can you be very discreet, muppets?

Very?

All right, I'll tell you.

Reusable Orc shirts.

That's right! It's the most amazing thing. You don't even need to wash them; you just run them through a simple dry-clean cycle (preferably on the slopes of Mount Doom) and they come out as clean as ever. And *such* a great wear factor! I declare, I can't *think* of the last time I've had such a triumph. He was quite taken aback, I can tell you! He didn't know what to say.

Speaking of which, I was telling you about the robes I designed for him. Crinoline, but with a bit of silk trim around the bottom to emphasize the sort of, I don't know, *swishiness* about him when he moves. And velvet patterns on the sleeves.

Now, I know all of this will probably be eaten up in the Final Battle with those *awful* people from Minas Tirith, but what I say is, it never hurts to go out looking your best.

Speaking of all this takes me back to the point I started with: the Battle of Five Armies. I was seriously nervous about the designs for that day, but in the end it all worked out. I mean, of course the goblins and Orcs and Wargs and so on were defeated and it was a terrible loss for Our Side, but the important thing was that we all looked our best. Isn't that the greatest part of any battle? Who'd have remembered the Battle of Dagorlad Plains if the Orcs hadn't been dressed to the nines as they charged the Elf ranks? Who'd really have remembered the Battle of the Pelennor Fields if the Orcs hadn't been in their very snazziest battle armor? The fact that they were slaughtered during the battle isn't important. They had clean underwear. That's what counts.

Now a word or two about wearing white after Midsummer's Eve. Don't.

That's my advice. Just don't. It's a shocking breach of etiquette, and no one ever does it except for a few irritating white wizards and the Witch of the Golden Wood. The correct dress is black. Plain black. With the occasional sequin or silk ribbon, but nothing more.

That's all from me, pumpkins! I've got to get back to work on the most cunning dress robes you ever *saw* for Wormtongue!

The Sackville-Baggins' Guide to Good Manners

What is the essence of good manners? Simply put, it is yielding to those of superior class the position in society that is rightfully theirs. If everyone obeyed that rule, the result would be an ordered, well-run society in which nothing ever happens and nothing ever changes. And who can argue with that?

As the Sackville-Bagginses—undoubtedly the most respected, well-born, widely known family in the Shire—can attest with extreme certainty, manners make the hobbit. This fact can be traced from the family's earliest ancestors who crossed the Brandywine and settled in what is now the Shire; such a momentous undertaking would have been unthinkable without the application not only of good manners among the inhabitants (for hobbits have few laws, and what ones they do have are, alas, too seldom enforced by the group of lazy, good-for-nothing sheriffs who spend all their time lollygagging around the Green Dragon). Manners were essential to the early hobbits who hacked out a life from the wilds that eventually became the Shire, but also important was a sense of *class*—and understanding that some are naturally born to rule and others to serve.

Manners will certainly get you places, and the Sackville-Bagginses, as the natural leaders of the Shire, are the shining epitome of manners. In fact, good manners and good breeding are a natural feature of this most noble of hobbit families. Otho Sackville-Baggins, for instance, can trace his family back for fifteen generations, and unlike his cousin Bilbo, there is none of that regrettable Took blood, which has led to such unfortunate incidents in the present and, apparently, the succeeding generations.

The quality of the Sackville-Baggins lineage can be recognized immediately in the regularity (nay, beauty) of their features as well as by the beauty of their language. Who better, then, to set the example for proper etiquette and behavior? If you are one of those unfortunate creatures that lacks the natural advantages of wit, looks, and general cleverness, take heed of the following.

TABLE MANNERS

Let us begin with proper conduct at the table.

Hobbits are a hungry people. Food is a passion, and they eat a minimum of six meals a day. That said, one would think there would be a better understanding among common hobbits of the proper manners that should be shown. Here, briefly, is a list.

1. **The menu should be planned in anticipation of the tastes of the most important guest.** It is the responsibility of other hobbits in attendance to cater to *his* sensibilities, not the other way around. Your true hobbit of sophistication and refinement prefers wine to beer, and sautéed dishes to fried ones, and never, ever, eats a parsnip. Meat should be well seasoned, vegetables should be of the freshest possible variety, and in particular potatoes (*not* "taters," as some vulgar hobbits insist upon calling them) should be peeled and diced, not cooked in their skins, which is characteristic of the lower classes of hobbit. All foods should be served in a succession of courses, not brought to the table at the same time. This enables the food to complement the conversation; in too many circumstances, hobbits insist on cramming their mouths with food and attempting to speak through it. This is both vulgar and disgusting.

2. **Guests should be seated in the order of importance.** The most significant guest, as determined by the age of his lineage and his social standing in the Shire, as well as his wealth and superior manners, should be seated at the top right end place of the table, next to the host. A cushion should be placed on his chair, elevating him above the other diners, and his glass should always be filled before anyone else's. If possible, a servant should stand behind him and cut up any particularly tough pieces of meat, as well as making sure that his glass is filled and that he has anything he should require. His wife should be seated several seats further down the table but above the wives of other guests.

3. **When the most important guest speaks, everyone else should fall silent, including the host, and listen to what he has to say.** They should refrain from chewing, swallowing, belching, shuffling their feet, coughing, blowing their noses, clearing their throats, or glancing at their watches.

4. **Knives belong on the left, forks on the right.** I *cannot* understand why this perfectly simple rule is not more widely observed in the Shire. Certain hobbits—whose names will remain unmentioned—have been observed at the Floating Log actually eating only with their knives! Eating *peas*! With a *knife*! Such is the sad state of our society today. (This, of course, is better than some reprobates, who attempt to eat all of their meals with their fingers alone. Shocking! Quite shocking!)

5. **When the meal is concluded, the host calls upon the Most Important Guest to propose a final toast.** The toast should be given with wine, not ale, since the drinking of ale is vulgar. Polite hobbit society drinks wine. Low,

public-house hobbits drink ale. That is an important distinction between the two social classes. The best wine is Old Winyards, of which the regrettable Bilbo appears to have a large supply.

6. **All food should be chewed with the mouth closed.** One should not take a drink of wine until one has thoroughly chewed what is in one's mouth. One should average twenty chews to the bite and avoid clicking the teeth together when chewing. One should not allow the tongue to emerge from the mouth and lick the lips (or anywhere else).

7. **If food falls on the floor, it is no longer edible and should be ignored.** It is disturbing to see how many hobbits apparently think that brushing the dirt off a morsel of chicken makes it fit to pop into their mouths. I cannot imagine how some of them have avoided falling ill.

8. **It should go without mentioning that speaking when one's mouth is full is impermissible under any circumstances.** Attempting to speak in dumb show—for instance, bouncing up and down in one's seat, waving one's arms to signal that one has something important to say—is equally gauche.

9. **It is polite to compliment the host on the food.** Something along the lines of, "This meat wasn't at all as bad as what you served the last time I ate with you," or "The mashed potatoes had a bit of flavor; you must have a new supplier," are always appreciated.

10. **When the meal is concluded, the well-bred hosts will offer the guests bowls of water in which to dip their hands.** Do *not* under any conditions use a bowl that has been used by one of your fellow guests. This is the invariable

sign of low breeding. Further, some lower-class hobbits appear to confuse finger bowls with washing basins and plunge their entire faces into the bowl. If any guest does this, he should be quickly and quietly escorted to the door and told never to come back.

11. **It is vulgar in the extreme to refer to the number of your guests as a "gross" or a "hundredweight."** This implies you've chosen them merely to fill out a required number, and no one appreciates that. In fact, no polite hobbit should use such expressions—they smack of a low, shop-keeping mind.

12. **During an after-dinner speech, the polite guest or host never does anything unexpected or surprising.** Certainly he does *not*, after a lot of ridiculous nonsense about how much he'll miss everyone and how much he esteems his friends and family, simply vanish without warning.

POLITE FORMS OF ADDRESS

We now turn to the proper way one should address another hobbit. The folk of the Shire do not have nobility and therefore abjure formal titles such as "Your Grace," "Your Highness," "Your Excellency," or "Your Muchitude." On formal occasions, "Sir" or "Madam" is acceptable. Sadly, the younger generation has fallen into the habit of addressing their elders merely as "Dad"—a disgraceful turn of events. In letters, the usual way to address a hobbit is to append to his name the name of the house he inhabits, assuming it to be noteworthy. Thus, one might address a letter to *Bolfur of Water's Fall, Hobbiton, The Shire.*

Speaking of letters, the increasing illiteracy among hobbits is a concern not to be ignored. Though there remain some who can write, it seems that the art of writing is falling into disuse among the common hobbitry. Most are content to make a few scratches here and there and can barely sign their names in a legible fashion.

Of course, there are a few professional copyists still living in the Shire—given the number of wills, contracts, and other official documents that must be drawn up, we could hardly do without them. But the younger generation seems to have completely neglected their letters. Only a radical change in the educational system of the Shire can repair this deficiency. Several leading families, including the Sackville-Bagginses, have submitted proposals for education reform, only to see them ignored or rejected outright. Really, one does one's best, but it's sad to see the lower classes sink into a state of turpitude and ignorance when one is so ready to lend the benefit of one's experience and wisdom.

Letters, as it need hardly be said, should be written in sepia ink on a clean, well-scraped parchment or sturdy paper. Important words and phrases should be in red ink or gold. The signature should be worthy of the writer's social standing; if the correspondent is of a distinguished family, several graceful flourishes after the name are indicated.

SOME FURTHER GENERAL REMARKS ON MANNERS

A few observations on travel follow. Hobbits do not, as a rule, travel much and certainly not beyond the borders of their land. One or two may ride out as far as Bree, where there is a respectable inn called *The Prancing Pony*. But since Bree is a mixed community of hobbits and the Big People, no truly respectable hobbit families would be caught within its environs. Those who do so are mainly

Brandybucks—hardly exemplars of good breeding. Indeed, since that family lives on the borders of the Shire and has an unhealthy dose of Stoor blood gurgling through its veins (some members actually go out on the river in *boats*), one shouldn't be surprised by any outlandish thing they do. Brandy Hall is a most disreputable place, full of distant relations and dubious characters that no Hobbiton hobbits would let pass their threshold.

Of course, there is traveling within various parts of the Shire: to Buckleberry, to Bywater, to Bridgefields. In such travels, one should make sure that the inns are clean, well run, and inhabited only by a better class of hobbit. A hobbit of high standing would be shocked by some of the low, vulgar conversation—to say nothing of the drinking—that goes on in the common room of The Green Dragon.

At the inn, one should be unafraid to speak sternly to the landlord and let him know that only the best class of rooms will do, with *clean* bedding that has been thoroughly checked for vermin. Supper should be served in the room, and you should be undisturbed by any of the rest of the inn's company. Waiters should be clean and attentive and not speak until spoken to.

At night, it may be best to leave several candles burning, just to give one a clear view of the door in case anyone tries to break in. It's best to bring one's own lock or, if none is available, push some piece of furniture against the door to discourage burglars.

Family Trees

A short comment on the subject of family trees follows. Outside observers have said that hobbits are "obsessed" with family and with tracing our ancestors back through countless generations. Nothing could be further from the truth.

In fact, very few hobbit families can trace their forebears more than a hundred years or so. It is precisely this that distinguishes good families from those of the lower elements. Respectable and proper hobbits keep their family genealogy carefully written out in red-bound books, marked in colored inks to show the casual observer the descent from father to son to son's son of the family name. Lower-class hobbits are usually content to stick up a sampler on the wall showing in crude stitching their line as far back as their grandparents. Such nonsense, needless to say, has no legal standing and may even serve to bring them into ridicule and contempt.

Of course, even the most respectable of hobbit families have the occasional scandal. One is hardly to blame if one's cousin goes off with a band of wandering dwarves, apparently by his own account, hired as a *thief*. And then, somehow, after fighting spiders and bears and elves and goodness knows what else (one gets in the habit of not listening closely to such nonsense), he goes and *burglarizes* the hoard of a dragon. A *dragon*! Really. What gibberish! There hasn't been a dragon seen anywhere close to the Shire in ... goodness knows how long. And yet, somehow, he defeats the dragon (as if that could ever happen) and comes back, accompanied by a raggedy wizard in dirty robes, and with a couple of chests of gold, if you please.

Naturally, one does one's best to put a good face on such things, as proper families do. The normal procedure with unwanted relatives is to ship them off somewhere quietly and ignore them until they have the good sense to die. However, sadly, this isn't always an option.

Instead, they stay around Hobbiton, throwing ridiculous and elaborate dinner parties, entertaining all sorts of outlandish guests, including some from over the borders, and making a spectacle in general. And, if you please, celebrating birthday after birthday, as if they meant to go on living forever, making life quite impossible for the normal members of the family.

Birthdays

Speaking of birthdays leads me to the proper etiquette for this custom. Because birthdays are such a feature of Shire life (there being at least one or two a week in these parts), this guide to manners would not be complete without a few comments about proper manners at a birthday party.

Invitations should be sent out at least a month in advance, written clearly and simply: So-and-so hobbit, esq., requests the pleasure of your company at his birthday party on such-and-such a date. Reply requested.

Greet guests at the door, dressed in your best clothing.

Here, too, one must remark on the sad decline of sartorial standards in our age. Gone are the days when a hobbit would no more dream of stepping outside without clean, well-pressed, and well-tended clothing than he would smoke a pipe filled with weeds from the garden. Today, strolling through Hobbiton, one is put off by the sight of old gaffers tending to their vegetable beds in old pants with patches on the knees and shirts coming out at the elbow. Surely any visitor from abroad making his way through the Shire today would conclude that he had happened upon a land devastated by some great natural disaster that had deprived the people of their clothing. It takes little or no effort to look clean and respectable, both for male and female hobbits. The latter are too inclined to wear scandalously revealing costumes, particularly those who serve ale in low taverns.

Proper hobbit wear consists of a shirt (white or gray), pants (dark brown or green), a waistcoat (*not* in some vulgar bright color but a discrete light blue or green embroidered with gold thread), and a jacket or topcoat (green, brown, or blue). The feet should be well brushed and trimmed; it's notable that many young hobbits these days are, apparently in some sort of fashion statement, wearing their foot hair long until they look as if they're carrying mops on the ends of their feet. This ridiculous affectation—mop feet—should excite the scorn of well-to-do hobbits throughout the Shire.

To return to the matter of birthday parties, it is customary at parties for the hobbit holding the party to give gifts to those in attendance. You may find it expedient to use gifts given at previous parties, but there is a feeling among some hobbits that the practice of "regifting" should be discouraged—or at least practiced with some discretion.

Some hobbits think it exciting to set off fireworks at parties. Fireworks are, above all, associated with wizards, which is why they should be strongly discouraged by those who wish to preserve the respectable character of the Shire. They are loud and showy and excite remark—just the things the upper class of hobbits should be seeking to avoid.

Wizards, as every hobbit knows, are nothing more than professional troublemakers. Ragged, itinerate, with long, white hair and flowing robes that bear the stains of travel, they wander in and out of the Shire without regulation. Apparently the border guards make no attempt to stop them, which is a sad comment on the porous nature of our border and reinforces one's vigorous call for increased border security and the expulsion of all illegal immigrants.

Wherever these wizards go, hobbit boys and girls are seduced by their stories of trolls, ogres, and dragons. A good many hobbits over the years have actually *left* the Shire in search of adventure—though none recently, not since the return of Bilbo Baggins fifty years ago.

IN SUMMATION

As this guide makes abundantly clear, we are living in an age of decline. The collapse of civilization as we know it may be only a few years away. But amid this chaos, families such as the Sackville-Bagginses stand as bedrocks against the tide of barbarism that is sweeping the land. They uphold the highest possible standards of morality and respectability and will serve as a beacon when all other lights go out.

They can do nothing less.

The Warg Whisperer

The Art of Training and Riding

the Giant Wolves of Middle-earth

nd in the middle of the circle was a great grey wolf. He spoke to them in the dreadful language of the Wargs. Gandalf understood it. Bilbo did not, but it sounded terrible to him, and as if all their talk was about cruel and wicked things, as it was. Every now and then all the Wargs in the circle would answer their grey chief all together, and then their dreadful clamour almost made the hobbit fall out of his pine-tree.

—From J.R.R. Tolkien's *The Hobbit*

A Warg is a fearsome creature. Known to prowl the mountains and foothills of Middle-earth in large packs, these animals should not be thought of as merely giant wolves. Wargs are an intelligent species capable of much more than simple wolf behavior (which can be complex in and of itself). For a moment, allow yourself to imagine the strength, cunning, and prowess of a gigantic wolf combined with heightened intelligence, a crude understanding of language, and the evil tendencies of the most corruptible of species—Man. You'll find that you'll envision a dangerous combination of traits indeed. And there you have the Warg.

Wargs measure roughly five feet at the shoulder and can reach up to ten feet in length from the tip of their snout to their tail. They have long necks and a muzzle full of fangs. Their eyes are small and located on each the side of the head, and the ears are swept back at the rear of the Warg's skull. It is thought that their eyes and ears evolved in this way to provide maximum sensory perception along with minimum vulnerability. Large and well muscled, Wargs are swift runners and are easily able to pounce upon and crush their prey. They have short fur in varying mottled patterns, which can aid in camouflage.

Warg society, much like that of normal wolves, is based on the pack mentality. A Warg pack or "tribe," as some refer to it, has a leader, though altercations to establish dominance are frequent.

While the Wargs are perfectly capable of their own plans and devices—often prowling the mountainous regions in search of prey large enough to be worth their time (Men, Elves, Dwarves, and the like)—they are often associated with goblins and Orcs, with whom they have an unsavory alliance. Orcs and goblins are known to ride on the backs of the wild Wargs, using them as sinister canine transport with the ability to track their enemies down. Wargs make ferocious mounts and have been known to turn on their riders. This is not surprising considering they are also known to turn on members of their own pack.

In spite of the danger, a Warg can make an excellent mount in battle if you are capable of controlling the beast. The creature becomes more than just a mode of travel—in the right hands, a Warg can be a weapon.

THE ANATOMY OF THE WARG

- **Eyes:** As previously mentioned, a Warg's eyes are positioned, more or less, on the sides of the animal's head. Such positioning provides the beast with the ability to see most of its perimeter. As a rider, the safest position is directly behind the Warg's head, being wary of times when it moves its neck (which is highly flexible). Try to keep the reins taut so the beast must focus forward in battle. Only allow it to move its head when it is completely focused on your enemy.

- **Ears:** As previously mentioned, a Warg's ears are positioned at the back of the head. In the thick of battle it will hear you more keenly than anything else going on around it. This can work to your advantage, as you may communicate simple directives and commands to the beast. It can also be a disadvantage if the Warg decides to turn on you or if you say the wrong thing. Know that your Warg can hear you, and never assume that it can't understand what you're saying.

- **Neck:** Wargs have long, prehensile necks, which are capable of a wide range of motion. This makes them excellent in battle, as they can easily snap at enemies around them with their strong jaws. The disadvantage is that, should they become angry with you, they can easily get their head turned toward you for an attack. Be ever vigilant.

- **Muzzle:** The muzzle of the Warg is equipped with rows and rows of teeth. While the muzzle can be used to direct the Warg while riding, the bridle and reins are typically adapted to allow full use of the animal's teeth as a weapon. So it's important to remember that even though the Warg may be equipped with some sort of riding harness, this likely won't afford you any protection from the beast's fangs.

- **Jaws:** It is important to respect the sheer muscle power behind the snapping jaws of a Warg. While the beast's teeth, like those of any canine, are not remarkably sharp to the touch and are often worn and rounded at the point, the powerful jaws more than make up for any dullness. In fact, the bite of the Warg can be even more painful because of this fact. Imagine the pain of being stabbed with dozens of small, dull daggers with the force of a steel trap. Most folks would prefer being gouged by a sharpened dragon talon any day of the week.

- **Nose:** Wargs, like other members of the canine family, have sensitive noses and keen senses of smell. This trait makes them very effective at tracking enemies in battle. Once a Warg gets on a scent, it cannot be deterred—it will find its prey.

- **Claws:** Sturdy claws and a sizable dewclaw allow Wargs to dig into their prey and cling to them in a way that most canines are unable to do. The claws also make formidable slashing weapons.

- **Paws:** A Warg's paw is a powerful weapon on its own. Their paws are massive and heavy; getting hit with one feels like being clubbed with a war-hammer—with claws.

- **Haunches:** The powerful haunches of Wargs allow them to run swiftly and jump great distances. They often take down large prey—such as a deer or horse—by launching themselves through the air to land on its back. Using the same tactic in battle allows them to knock riders from their mounts before eviscerating them and gobbling them up.

- **Chest:** Wargs have broad, muscular chests that allow them to launch full-frontal attacks on their prey. Impact with a Warg's chest is like running into a fur-coated brick wall.

ARMOR & PROTECTIVE CLOTHING

As a potential Warg rider, you'll need to think about protecting yourself, not only from the enemies you'll face in battle, but from your mount itself. It is recommended that you wear some form of armor—various types may work, but there are advantages and disadvantages to every sort.

- **Mail:** Mail armor will certainly help defend against cuts and puncture wounds that you may receive from a Warg bite or an errant claw, and wearing mail as an undergarment is, indeed, a good idea. The downside of mail is that it likely won't provide much protection from the sheer pressure of a Warg bite, so you'll still suffer some tissue damage—some bruising at the very least. It also won't guard against any blunt strikes from the creature's extremities.

- **Plate Armor:** Full plate armor certainly can offer more protection from an assortment of strikes—be they from your enemies or from your wolfish mount. The downside to plate armor is that it is cumbersome and can inhibit movement. What advantage you gain will likely be offset by the lack of mobility you'll experience sitting in the saddle fully armored.

- **Leather:** Many Warg riders prefer leather armor because it is less bulky. Leather armor, particularly chaps, riding boots, and riding gloves, can be very effective and affords you greater mobility. Of course, you'll be more vulnerable to arrows and blades from the enemies you face in battle.

Ultimately you may choose to mix and match your armor from these selections—which is smart. Try out different pieces and see how they hinder your movement (it will be different for every rider).

A good strategy is to bulk up in highly exposed areas, such as the back and chest, but use lighter armor for your arms, legs, and waist.

TAMING & TRAINING A WARG

Admittedly, the title of this section is a bit of a joke because Wargs can never be truly tamed. The best you can hope for is a tentative alliance with the beast: You have an enemy and the Warg shares that enemy, and so you are joined together in your hatred. When approaching your relationship with a Warg you intend to ride, it is very important to keep this dynamic in mind.

Respect the animal's intelligence; talk to it as an equal. Offerings of food may help, but do not tender this offering as you would with any ordinary animal. Wargs understand that gifts are not given freely, and any offering you make will be suspect. Make your intentions known through words or gestures. Talking gently to a Warg—as you might with some other creature (a horse or mule, for example)—will not serve you. It may even enrage the creature, as it may see your attempts to soothe it as an act of condescension. Getting into a Warg's good graces is best done by approaching the creature as you would a potential partner or ally. Communicate to the creature that you wish to ride it, and make it known what purpose your partnership will ultimately serve. How much a Warg understands typically depends on the individual, but one thing is certain—Wargs hate a common enemy. Use that to your advantage.

Training the Warg is a task you'll want to approach carefully. Wargs are intelligent creatures and will respond well to many different types of commands: verbal commands, gestures, and touch commands. But while they are quite intelligent and very capable of understanding commands, tactics, and some limited strategy, they are also quite unpredictable. While training the Warg for riding and battle, it is important to remind the creature of your mutual goal and treat the animal as a partner, rather than a beast of burden.

Warg Training Tips

- Food may be used as a motivator.

- Talk to the animal respectfully, as you would to a partner, rather than treating it like a pet.

- Use simple commands, whether verbal or gestured. Wargs have a limited understanding of language (but never assume they do not understand you).

- Show no fear.

Make sure you project confidence and a strong will. Wargs respect strength and power, so it is important to show no fear. This does not mean you should try to dominate the creature. Such action will likely provoke retaliation on the creature's behalf.

FEEDING YOUR WARG

The Warg diet is not very complicated. It consists of hunks of meat. Wargs are predators, but they are also scavengers—so the meat in question may, in fact, be, well, in question. Fresh meat dripping in blood or rotting hunks of flesh covered in flies—either way, your Warg won't starve.

And as to the kind of meat? No worries there either. Any kind of meat will do, really—deer, rabbit, lamb, Dwarf, hobbit, human—it doesn't matter.

Given that Wargs are hunters and are used to bringing down their prey in the wild, when making your first appeal to a Warg with food, you may want to simulate a fresh kill. The meat should be butchered roughly. Organ meats (heart, kidneys, liver) are the first to be eaten in the wild, so to really "make friends," try offering those parts to the Warg first. Joining the Warg in eating some of the organ meat yourself is a good idea as well. It shows that you are not simply deferring to the Warg. You send a message that you are approaching the beast as an equal.

RIDING TACTICS

Riding a Warg isn't like riding your typical mount. Let's face it; this isn't a pony ride. The beast can move in a manner that your typical horse cannot. A Warg can easily zig, zag, cut, and dart, making it very useful in battle but also a nightmare to stay on. You might as well try riding a wild steer bareback with nothing more than a rope and a glove to stay mounted—and that's just crazy. But there it is. Riding a Warg isn't an activity for the faint of heart.

To ride, you need to be in peak physical condition. Your arm muscles need to be strong in order to hold on. Your legs should be conditioned so that you can squeeze and clamp down on the beast, digging your ankles in to stay on. Your core muscles should be strong to keep your insides on the inside. A Warg will try to throw you off or at least shake your guts loose inside your body. Prepare yourself through a strict regimen of calisthenics, including push-ups, pull-ups, sit-ups, crunches, squats, leg raises, planks, and the like. Repeat often.

As for your riding strategy and tactics that you might employ in battle, keep in mind that the Warg has many advantages that a horse or other mount does not. The creature is much more maneuverable (when it chooses to obey your commands). The range of motion a Warg is capable of at high speeds makes it effective as both a mount and a weapon.

Riding in Battle

A few things to keep in mind when riding a Warg in battle:

- Keep your focus forward. Your Warg will be fighting whatever enemies are in its path. If your attention wanders, you may find that the creature has engaged an enemy on its own. When on Warg-back, the goings-on of the battle behind you should be a secondary concern at best. (And, yes, this makes you a target from behind ... so consider some good back armor.)

- A lance or spear may be effective for the lead charge in a battle, but you may want to quickly abandon it in favor of a sword, axe, or cudgel. Once engaged in combat, your Warg's quick darting motions will make long weapons—like a lance or spear—unwieldy and much less effective.

- Be ready to bail out. You're likely to get thrown, period. If you're prepared for it, you might lessen the blow. Be ready to find yourself in the middle of the melee on foot. It's a good idea to strap on a few extra weapons—especially smaller ones, such as short swords, small axes, or daggers.

TACK & EQUIPMENT

Make sure your saddle, reins, and harnesses are all in good condition. Failure to do so can have disastrous ramifications. You want to minimize the risk of being thrown from your animal—especially in the heat of battle.

- **Saddle:** Similar to a horse's saddle, you'll strap your Warg saddle to the beast's back and fasten it around its middle using a wide strap, known as a *cinch*. The cinch should be positioned a few inches behind the animal's front legs. It is important to make sure the saddle fits properly. If the saddle causes the Warg discomfort, the creature will turn on you. If the saddle is too loose or too tight, it may malfunction, resulting in injury or death—likely yours, not the Warg's.

- **Breastplate:** This device, which fastens to the saddle and covers the Warg's chest, may prevent the saddle from shifting during your ride.

- **Stirrups:** Similar to stirrups used for horseback riding, these footholds hang to either side of the saddle. They may provide greater stability for your ride, but many Warg riders opt not to use them because too often a rider will be thrown, get a foot caught in a stirrup, and find himself dragged by the beast.

- **Bridle:** Unlike a horse's bridle, the headgear for a Warg does not have a bit. The beast would simply chew through it, and it would also detract from its usefulness in battle—a Warg's fangs can (and should) be used as a weapon. The Warg bridle is comprised of simple straps around the head to which reins are attached.

- **Reins:** These leather straps attach to the bridle and are used to convey directional commands to the Warg. Similar to the reins you'd use for a horse, the reins can be pulled to either side to "steer" the beast. Pulling back on the reins conveys the desire to stop—but don't count on it happening. As previously mentioned, the reins for a Warg are not attached to a bit of any kind. The Warg will feel you tugging, and with training it should know what your commands mean. Whether or not it chooses to obey your commands is another matter entirely. Hold tight to the reins and hope for the best.

WARG WEAKNESSES

Wargs are powerful, maneuverable, and smarter than most beasts. That doesn't mean they are without weaknesses. They are animals first and foremost, so they can become distracted in battle by anything perceived as food. Be aware that your Warg may decide to devour a fallen enemy in the midst of battle rather than turning to fight other attackers. This tendency can put you and your Warg in harm's way. Feeding your mount before going into battle can help avoid this problem.

Wargs are especially afraid of fire. This is a key weakness among the species. A well-prepared enemy will be aware of this weakness and attempt to use fire against you in battle. Training your Warg to withstand his fear of flame can be effective but is also a dangerous proposition. Use extreme care and work slowly so the beast does not turn against you. Providing protective armor for the Warg can also help lessen the creature's fear of fire.

YOU & YOUR WARG

Accept the fact that you and your Warg will never be friends. Unlike a horse or a dog or some other kind of animal, a Warg will not bond with you, and no allegiance will ever develop between you and the beast. The relationship you have with the animal is the same as you might have with your sword or mace. Work with the Warg as you would with any weapon used in battle: Treat it with care and respect, and always make sure you know which way the sharp end is pointed.

Notes on Spying From the Crebain

CREBAIN INFORMATION AGENCY (CIA)

"Spying Is Our Business"

MEMO

FROM: 1st Secretary, 2nd Division, 6th Protocol, Section R.iv/NJC

TO: 11th Secretary, 9th Division, 43rd Protocol, Section WW.xii/YBF

This memo is to notify you that your division is *once again* tardy with its TPS reports. This marks the eleventh time in twelve weeks that your TPS reports have been filed late or without proper covering signatures. Note that *all intelligence reports must have proper covering signatures* according to the new procedures memo concerning TPS reports (Mem.6a/1D4&16.wff/J). If you require a copy of this memo, it will be forwarded to you. Meanwhile, please let me have all TPS reports for this month in triplicate as required with proper signatures. If I do not receive these by 15:30 hours, severe disciplinary measures will be taken.

CC: CIA 1st Minister; file

MEMO

FROM: 11th Secretary, 9th Division, 43rd Protocol, Section WW.xii/YBF

TO: 1st Secretary, 2nd Division, 6th Protocol, Section R.iv/NJC

Sorrysorrysorrysorrysorry! It won't happen again. I swear it. I got behind in paperwork, what with the upcoming war. Don't we make any exceptions for stress in times of national emergency? Could I ask for an extension of twenty-four hours on the TPS reports? I'll get them done on time in the future. Really. Please.

CC: File

MEMO

TO: 11th Secretary, 9th Division, 43rd Protocol, Section WW.xii/YBF

FROM: 1st Secretary, 2nd Division, 6th Protocol, Section R.iv/NJC

Your request for a twenty-four extension in the filing time for your TPS reports has been reviewed and is hereby rejected. As was remarked in the previous communication, the failure to properly file these reports has been a consistent pattern in your case, and I am unable to accept your assurances that this deficiency will be corrected in the future. We do not make any exceptions for national emergencies. The impending conflict makes it all the more important that detailed intelligence reports be promptly filed with all attendant Protocol. Your wittering on this issue has only reduced the time available to you for the proper filing of the back reports. I remind you that I must have these in hand by 15:30 hours or significant change will be contemplated in your current assignment.

CC: CIA 1st Minister; file

MEMO

FROM: 11th Secretary, 9th Division, 43rd Protocol, Section WW.xii/YBF

TO: 1st Secretary, 2nd Division, 6th Protocol, Section R.iv/NJC

What sort of change?

CC: File

MEMO

TO: 11th Secretary, 9th Division, 43rd Protocol, Section WW.xii/YBF

FROM: 1st Secretary, 2nd Division, 6th Protocol, Section R.iv/NJC

You have inquired as to the nature of a possible change in your current assignment, resulting from your failure to maintain a timely filing of TPS reports. Please keep in mind that information gathering here in Hollin is widely considered "easy duty" within the agency, since the land is largely uninhabited (save by animals) and barren, and there is little need for more than routine information surveys. There are places that present considerably greater challenges. Think Imladris.

CC: CIA 1st Minister; file

MEMO

FROM: 11th Secretary, 9th Division, 43rd Protocol, Section WW.xii/YBF

TO: 1st Secretary, 2nd Division, 6th Protocol, Section R.iv/NJC

Not Imladris! We'll get the reports done! I swear! Crebain *never* come back from Imladris. We'll get the reports out to you by 15:30 hours. By 15:00 hours! By 14:00!

CC: File

MEMO

TO: 11th Secretary, 9th Division, 43rd Protocol, Section WW.xii/YBF

FROM: 1st Secretary, 2nd Division, 6th Protocol, Section R.iv/NJC

I am in receipt of your back TPS reports. While appreciative of your industry in filing these reports earlier than requested, I must point out that they contain a shocking lack of detail, as well as numerous spelling and grammatical errors. I cannot, in good conscience, pass them on to the Higher Information Review and Assessment Working

Group (HIRAWAG) until these issues have been addressed. Moreover, HIRAWAG is unlikely to grant any further extension to your already overshot deadline for filing these reports.

Therefore, you are instructed to take the following steps:

1. Revise the attached TPS reports for correct grammar and spelling.

2. Indicate in places marked the details requested, including complete lists of all suspicious and nonsuspicious activity within the time periods indicated. Note that the forms as currently completed do not contain this essential information.

I shall expect these revisions on my desk by no later than 18:30. For your reference, I attach a copy of the CIA Training Manual Number 42/6-jscII/:li, which will refresh you in the basics of Crebain information-gathering technique. I do this with some reluctance, since the material in the manual is of a basic nature and should already be known to you, but it seems clear that you and your subordinates have become significantly forgetful of its tenets. Please review it thoroughly and keep the information in mind in respect to all future activities.

Consider this a favor on my part. A stricter secretary would have already consigned you to duties on the borders of Imladris, at the mercy of Elven archers. What your chances there would be, given your apparent lack of basic intelligence-gathering skills, I scarcely like to think. I can only implore you, then, to take seriously the crafting of your TPS reports and the mastery of this manual.

CC: File

CREBAIN INFORMATION AGENCY (CIA)

"Spying Is Our Business"

Training Manual Number 42/6-jscII/:li

Introduction

Spying and the collection of information, particularly by aerial survey, has been the providence of the Crebain from time immemorial. The charge was first given the agency in the First Age by Morgoth himself. It is therefore incumbent upon all Crebain to bear in mind at all times the awful responsibility entrusted to us. In our talons lies the future of Middle-earth.

Overview

Spying should be considered an art, not a trade. Intelligence is not merely a collection of techniques; at its center lies the power of imagination. It is not enough to merely report what an enemy is doing and where he is going. The skilled analyst should be able to anticipate from available information what the enemy is *going* to do and where he is *going* to do it. What is required is, at times, a leap of vision, more intuitive than mechanical.

Basic Principles

The primary basis of Crebain information gathering lies in aerial reconnaissance. The power of such surveys lies in their ability to scout a large area at once and to detect various targets within it. Through this, it is entirely possible to discover forces that are quite unaware of one another's existence, although they may be passing as little as a few hundred feet from one another.

Surveys should be taken using the following methods.

1. The ideal height for effective surveillance is between 100 and 150 feet. At this height, the intelligence agent is able to survey a wide range of territory while being relatively immune from attacks by anyone or anything on the ground. (Important note: If surveying near any Elven party or settlement, height should be increased to a minimum of 300 feet.)

     a. This instruction should be modified in the event of cloud cover. In such cases, it is recommended to fly just below the clouds, which provide a ready means of concealment in the event of discovery.

2. In a sky marked by scattered clouds, it is essential to always move *with the wind*. An object moving against the wind is easily detectable.

3. If at all possible, flight pattern should be one of concentric circles, moving from left to right, each circle approximately 1,000 to 1,500 feet in diameter.

     a. Within twenty to twenty-five minutes after the first flight, a second flight, moving and circling in the opposite direction, should re-cover the ground.

4. Crebain surveying is carried out by Protocols, and never by individual fliers, to prevent the possibility of false sightings or incorrect interpretation of data.

5. Low-flying patrols are launched under special circumstances, when it is necessary to make a more detailed observation of a designated object. Such patrols must first be au-

thorized under Protocol Guidelines Section IV-c, paragraph I., subsection XIX. (Files in triplicate to be sent to Division headquarters.)

a. Low-flying patrols are to make their observations of a height no higher than 20 feet and as low as 5 feet.

b. Such patrols are not to exceed speeds of five wing beats per second.

c. Low fliers are to make only one approach to the subject within an eight-hour period to avoid raising suspicions of observation.

d. Data collected from such observations is to be entered on Form TPS/iii/1040a-20 and filed in quadruplicate with Divisional and Secretariat officials (see Handbook D/Rip-iv/2.365: *Proper Filing of Forms).*

6. In certain exceptional circumstances it may be permissible to make observations while perching. The following guidelines apply:

a. Permission to Perch forms are to be completed and submitted *at least* twenty-four hours before the perching begins.

b. Permission to Perch forms must be approved unanimously at the Secretariat level.

c. Perching is to be done for no more than three consecutive minutes at a distance of no less than 10 feet from the Object of Observation.

d. All perching observations are to be submitted within twelve hours of the completion of the perching.

Objects of Observation

The broad intent of observation is to gather information on the movement of unauthorized individuals, whether traveling alone or in company. Observations may also be taken of weather conditions, geographic events (e.g., earthquakes, volcanic eruptions, forest fires, etc.), battles, or other large-scale events. Among the most important objects of observation are the following:

1. Travelers. Travelers often move in small packs, normally on foot with accompanying horses or ponies used as pack animals. Although most are of little concern (being abroad on personal or commercial errands), some few may be of interest; the task of determining whether their travel is of intelligence interest should be left to analysts and is not the providence of those gathering observations. Of particular interest are those travelers who:

  a. move off established roads or trails

  b. visit old ruins/fortresses/cave entrances

  c. move in a direction that would indicate they intend to visit a stronghold of the Enemy (e.g., Imladris, Lórien, Rohan)

2. Elves. All Elves are to be kept under observation at all times, whether moving singly or in packs. For the most part, Elves in large groups will tend to move westward, toward the Grey Havens. Nonetheless, they should be closely observed, and proper reports should be filed in a timely manner. Any Elves leaving Imladris or Lórien should be subject to a Class A/3 grade level of coverage, reports to be filed twice daily.

a. Note: Since Elves are noted for their skill with bows, extreme caution is advised when conducting observations. Please note that if you are wounded and fall into Elvish hands, the CIA will disavow any knowledge of your activities.

3. **Rangers.** Rangers are subject to Class A/6b grade level of coverage. Their general area of concentration is in the North, to the west of the Anduin. A number have been sighted in close proximity to a small, unimportant area called The Shire (see Appendix K/23Jrb-3.6, Maps–Northwest). Rangers, because they are of an ancient race, the Númenoreans, are skilled in the ways of the Wild and therefore present particular problems with observation. They are farsighted and will recognize Crebain from a great distance. It is therefore recommended that aerial observation be exclusively employed in tracking their movements at a minimal height of 500 feet.

(Handwritten note: It has been rumored for some time that a special segment of Rangers may have dedicated themselves to tracking down and silencing any who are deemed to be spying on their movements. This group—known as the Númenorean Security Arm (NSA)—should be further investigated and closely watched.)

4. **Dwarves.** Because of their short stature, Dwarves move slowly and present no particular tracking and observational challenges. Their weapon of choice is the axe, one that is unthreatening to Crebain except when perched. *(Handwritten note: True that! Even then, Dwarves make so much*

noise and their breath smells so much like stale beer that any Crebain who can't get out of the way of the swing of a Dwarvish axe deserves what's coming to him.) The greatest challenge Dwarves present to accurate observation is their penchant for going underground when things above ground get difficult. In the event that a band of Dwarves disappears beneath the ground, further observation must be turned over to the sixth section of our sister organization, Mordor Intelligence (MI6), for continued tracking via bats, fish, snakes, etc.

5. **Men.** These are among the easiest Objects of Observation, since they are generally the stupidest (though the Dwarves run a close second). They usually move in packs, often with a great deal of fuss and noise, setting up camp in the open with large fires that mark their place in the landscape. They pay little attention to the world around them, being far too absorbed in themselves and so are little likely to mistake a Crebain Protocol for anything more than a flock of annoyingly loud birds. All forms of observation have been authorized against Men, whether traveling through the Wild or in one of their cities (see below for rules on city-based observation). In short, the danger in observing Men is that they may generate too much information, occasionally making it difficult to separate the wheat from the chaff.

6. **Animals.** Movement of animals of all kinds is to be included in Protocol reports, since such occurences may signal something important or may itself be of consequence. This particularly includes the movement of horses, ponies, and other sorts of animals that are used for transportation; it also in-

cludes the movement of oliphaunts, giant spiders, and other beasts of war. It applies as well to the movement of small animals—no animal is too small to escape the observation of a well-trained and well-supervised Protocol. Animal-based observation is the bread and butter of good intelligence. It can show far more than the flashier observations of Rangers and wizards.

(Handwritten note: Yes, but it's a lot more boring.)

7. Huorns. Huorns are semisentient trees that move quickly and under cover of a created darkness, usually under the supervision of Ents, another set of treelike entities. Because Huorns are unpredictable and potentially extremely dangerous, all Perching and Low-Flying missions are never to be carried out in their vicinity.

(Note: A memorial exists in the central CIA office to the gallant Crebain of the 13th Division, 25th Protocol, who attempted a flight through Fangorn Forest in pursuit of a wizard and were never heard from again. May their memories remain ever black in our hearts!)

8. Wizards. Although wizards generally travel alone and may be sometimes mistaken for Men, nothing could be further from the truth. In point of fact, they are among the most challenging Objects of Observation. First, they are experienced in the art of concealing themselves. A wizard often blends in with the landscape, although a keen-eyed Crebain can still see him, particularly when he moves. Second, wizards are skilled at woodcraft; they know how to travel at night and conceal signs of their passing. Third, they have a preternatural sense of when they are being watched, and since they are fully aware of the existence of the CIA and of the nature of our mission—unlike many of the others mentioned above—they can select circumstances that make it excessively difficult for us to make direct observations. For these reasons, all wizards are subject to Class A/1 grade observation, and all reports on their movements and activities are to be forwarded *immediately* to the Secretariat, copies to Division head and to file in quintuplicate. Any wizard moving into or on the borders of Mordor will signal a Level 3 Defensive Condition, with appropriate responses from all Divisions and Protocols (see Handbook L/Pin-vi/8.3lj_6: *DefCons 1–6: Proper Procedures and Authorities*).

City-Based Observation

Although most Crebain intelligence work is carried out in the Wild, it may occasionally become necessary for Protocols to make city-based observations. Such observations must be preapproved at the Secretariat level and be of specified limited duration. Protocols entering an urban environment do so not as a group but as individuals, later congregating at a preset rendezvous point for comparison of observations. Otherwise, contact should be kept to a minimum. Rather, members of the Protocol should seek to find listening posts from which intelligence can be obtained (near windows or on the roofs of important buildings such as palaces, military barracks, etc.) and should attempt to form networks and recruit agents from among the city's native birds.

[Note: Under all circumstances, avoid contact with ravens. They have been determined to generally favor the Dwarves and are, at best, indifferent to the cause of the East. Swallows and thrushes are also generally immune to offers for intelligence, and sparrows have so little native brain power that they are, for all intents and purposes, useless for any but the most obvious news. The best subjects are starlings, who have a strong, natural tendency toward Mordor.]

Once such agents have been placed, it may be valuable to attempt to insert one of them into the chambers of a high figure in the city, possibly as a pet. Such informers (or "moles") are particularly valuable as sources of inside intelligence. Placement of a mole may require long preparation, but the rewards are infinite. All information emanating from a mole is to be subject to special handling under Authority 6.35d/iv_SecC. It is to be delivered to the nearest collection center every twelve hours for immediate transmission to the Secretariat.

Protocols should not remain in the environs of the city for more than seventy-two hours. Members should leave individually and rendezvous at a point some distance away from the city so as not to raise suspicions.

Special Objects of Observation

Several areas and objects are subject to special observation. Protocols carrying out these assignments receive special training and can be joined by special application only (those wishing to inquire further must complete form TJR_3x/spec-assign/6.3jp—Complete top blue sheet *only*). These areas include:

1. **Imladris.** Ancient stronghold of the Elves, this deep dell in the lands to the west of the Misty Mountains is of particular interest to the intelligence services. Since it is guarded by large numbers of magical enchantments, as well as the bows of the Elves who inhabit it, it represents a highly dangerous and therefore glorious and prestigious assignment for any Crebain Protocol. All intelligence gained from the Imladris Protocols is subject to special handling under Authority 6.35d/iv_SecA. It is to be delivered to a Collection Center (see below).

2. **Minas Tirith.** As the most important city in Gondor (indeed, in all Middle-earth) and the seat of power most near Mordor, this city is under constant CIA observation. (See section on city-based observation.) Fortunately, a lengthy surveillance has meant city inhabitants have grown used to the sight of Crebain settling on city walls and towers, and they only occasionally attempt to drive them away with sticks and stones. The result has been a triumph of operational intelligence, one that has been recognized at the Highest Levels of Power.

3. **Lothlórien.** If Minas Tirith represents a victory for well-coordinated intelligence gathering, Lothlórien represents an abject failure. Even more than Imladris, it is hedged by Elvish enchantments, and those Protocols that have attempted to penetrate its borders have, to a bird, been lost. Our agents, therefore, have been reduced to flying patrols on the outskirts of the Golden Wood, picking up what little information can be gained from starlings and other loquacious birds that

are allowed to enter the forest. Such information, entered on Form LL-3.89jRJ/lg_C, is to be conveyed Eyes Only to the chief of the nearest collection center.

Collection Centers

All field reports (FRs) are to be delivered to the nearest collection center for processing and transmission to central headquarters. Such deliveries are to be made under conditions of *absolute secrecy* at a minimum of once every twenty-four hours (except when otherwise specified in this manual).

Reports will be handed over to a Keeper, who will ask for a password (password to be rotated daily); the Deliverer will give the password and request a response key, supplied by the Keeper. Only then will the reports be transferred. The Deliverer will remain at the collection center until such time as the first stage of processing has been completed.

> *[Note: All FRs must be covered by Time-Point Sheets (TPS). This is essential, and no FR will be accepted without a TPS. The TPS should include the time expended in obtaining and recording the intelligence and the points assigned to it in intelligence value. This is important, since it allows the agency an accurate means of cost-benefit analysis and the ability to determine its work schedule and Objects of Observation to be targeted. Again, no FR will be accepted without an accompanying TPS, properly filled out and containing all requisite signatures.]*

The Nature of Crebain Observation

It cannot be stressed too strongly that the central object of the Crebain Information Agency is the *gathering* of intelligence. We do not seek to intervene in battle or affect the outcome of any event directly. It is therefore strictly forbidden for Crebain to interact with any of the Objects of Observation, other than by observing them.

It is understood that occasionally Crebain may be captured. In that case, the captured Crebain is instructed to commit suicide by means of the poisoned quill supplied to each Protocol member; there are *no exceptions* to this rule. If a Protocol member is captured, the secretary of the Protocol is required to complete form 18-J/Deceased-12viii/2.54 within twenty-four hours, it being assumed that the captive will have carried out his instructions and will be dead. The form will be submitted to superiors, who will then generate a standard letter of condolence to be delivered to the next of kin.

A further comment: Each Protocol operates on the principle of *shared information*. That is to say, all the Crebain within a Protocol constantly share and compare information. The intent is that each member of the Protocol knows exactly as much as his fellows; therefore the loss of any one or more members of the Protocol does not affect the information it is able to bring back from its mission.

MEMO

FROM: 11th Secretary, 9th Division, 43rd Protocol, Section WW.xii/YBF

TO: 1st Secretary, 2nd Division, 6th Protocol, Section R.iv/NJC

Okay, I read the manual and I went over the TPS reports again. I still don't see why they're so important. Can't you just let the Big Guy tell you what to watch and what not to watch? Why do we need all these forms and things to do that?

CC: File

MEMO

FROM: 1st Secretary, 2nd Division, 6th Protocol, Section R.iv/NJC

TO: 11th Secretary, 9th Division, 43rd Protocol, Section WW.xii/YBF

I am in receipt of your revised TPS reports and will soon send you a memo, evaluating your work in preparing them—perhaps I should say, in re-preparing them, considering the state of the first ones you turned in.

In regard to your observation concerning the value of TPS reports, not to mention the other forms mentioned throughout the manual and our other publications, I am, I confess, shocked and dismayed that a member of this organization could make such a statement. If the past thousand years have taught us one thing, it is that good intelligence work rests on a foundation of paperwork. Without clear records and constant record keeping, the magnificent accomplishments of this agency would be as nothing. In the end, if I may be permitted the observation, the intelligence you make is equal to the intelligence you take. The constant stream of valuable material that makes its way from our headquarters to our clients has been made possible by the traditions handed down to us from the past and tested over generations of our ancestors.

I trust you have learned this lesson and will apply it to your work in the future.

CC: File

MEMO

FROM: 1st Secretary, 2nd Division, 6th Protocol, Section R.iv/NJC

TO: 11th Secretary, 9th Division, 43rd Protocol, Section WW.xii/YBF

I have reviewed the TPS reports and other materials submitted with your most recent memo.

Please be advised that you are hereby immediately transferred to the Imladris Protocol, 32nd Division, 69th Protocol, Section XXL_SuddenDeath/RPC.

Please pick up a Next of Kin notification form on your way there.

CC: CIA 1st Minister; file

The Black Squirrels of Mirkwood

Adaptable, Resilient, and Kinda, Sorta Evil

here were black squirrels in the wood. As Bilbo's sharp inquisitive eyes got used to seeing things he could catch glimpses of them whisking off the path and scuttling behind tree-trunks ...

—From J.R.R. Tolkien's *The Hobbit*

In addition to fate and luck, survival is about opportunity and re-sources and maybe being just a little bit evil. Take a lesson from one of the most pervasive and successful species of the dark forest—the Black Squirrels of Mirkwood. You may ask: Can a squir-rel be truly evil? And that's a valid question. After all, isn't a squir-rel just a squirrel? Forget the creature you know today, with its cute twitching nose, bushy tail, and its tendency to run in the other direc-tion when humans approach. This is not the same animal. Just ask a group of silly Dwarves who once tried to eat a Mirkwood squirrel, and you might hear a different tale. Not one of harrowing escapes and near-death experiences—but one of a greasy, grisly, sinewy meal that *tasted* truly evil.

Evilness aside, these squirrels are a perfect example of adap-tation. Their very color gives insight into the clever nature of these resourceful creatures. Mirkwood's squirrels weren't always black; they originated with gray-brown fur, like that of any typical squirrel. Their color changed over time as the forest was corrupted by the dark magic of the Necromancer. As the wood grew deeper, darker, and more sinister, the squirrels' fur became blacker and blacker.

Isn't that spooky? Doesn't it just give you the willies? Personally I can't even look at an acorn without thinking about it, and it freaks me right the hell out.

This gradual and creepy adaptation of the squirrels' fur might be explained as a simple case of natural camouflage—much like the way a chameleon can change color to match its surroundings. But those who are wary or superstitious attribute the squirrels' coloration to the influence of the dark wizard. You can decide for yourself what to believe.

Mirkwood squirrels have also developed the capacity to understand language and have been known to act as spies—both for the Wood-elves who also live in the forest and for Sauron himself. These activities are most likely due to the squirrels' strong instincts toward self-preservation. The opportunistic nature of these animals is a large part of what makes them such a successful species. Never forget that squirrels are not devoted to anyone. This makes them highly unpredictable and not to be messed with.

To truly understand how cunning and adaptable (and quite possibly evil) the Mirkwood squirrels are, it's important to examine their attributes.

CLIMBING ABILITIES

Black squirrels can jump ten times their body length. Their ankles rotate nearly all the way around, allowing them superb climbing abilities no matter which direction their bodies are physically oriented. They are one of the only creatures that have the ability to climb down a tree headfirst. Now, if I described any other entity in such a manner, your very first thought would likely be of demonic possession. Am I right?

Because of their freakish speed and agility, these squirrels can deftly navigate the canopy of the dark Mirkwood forest and go unnoticed, which allows them to be the eyes and ears of the woods—making them perfect spies, messengers, and emissaries for dark deeds.

DIET

Have you ever seen a carnivorous squirrel? Mirkwood squirrels unfortunately cannot digest woody plant matter such as tree bark or twigs and therefore must rely on foods rich in carbohydrates, protein, and fat. For the most part they get their nutrients from nuts and seeds, but when these food sources germinate and sprout the squirrel cannot use them. And that's when things get crazy, because when these squirrels are really hungry they may devour insects, eggs, or even young birds, snakes, or rodents. And just ask yourself: Who's next?

SENSORY OVERLOAD

Have you ever seen a relaxed squirrel? It's a bit of an oxymoron. A squirrel is always hyperalert and on guard to the point of nervousness. This is even truer of the squirrels of the dark forest.

The black squirrels of Mirkwood have incredible eyesight. Their peripheral vision is as crisp as their focused vision. They can see things above and beside them without needing to move their heads. Their eyesight has also adapted to the darkness of the forests and is keen even in the complete absence of light.

At times, one would even think the creatures capable of seeing behind them, but I don't want to think about that for too long or I won't be able to sleep tonight. In all actuality, their heightened awareness can likely be attributed to the combination of all of their keen senses. Their hearing is nearly as acute as their eyesight. They can hear the smallest rustle or whisper within the radius of at least a mile. Their entire nervous system is tuned into their environment. They can sense subtle changes in temperature and pick up the faintest of scents on the breeze. Not much can happen in Mirkwood without the squirrels knowing about it.

STRENGTH, SPEED, & AGILITY

Proportional to their body size, these strange squirrels have amazing strength. Their compact bodies are made up almost entirely of muscle and sinew. They can pull themselves up onto a tree branch by a single toenail if need be. They navigate the winding forest paths quickly and make sharp, tight turns. A black squirrel is nearly impossible to catch. (Not that you would want to do that. Seriously, *why* would you want to do that?)

ADAPTABILITY

If all of that isn't enough to convince you that these creatures aren't on the level, let's talk about their uncanny ability to withstand almost anything Mother Nature can throw at them. The Mirkwood squirrels are highly adaptable. Their bodies easily adjust to extreme weather. In the winter they grow fat to retain warmth, and their coats become thicker and bushier. Their tails, which are highly vascular and contain an elaborate system of capillaries, serve to regulate their body heat as well. In the winter their tails help supply their bodies with warm blood, and in the summer the squirrels wick away their excess body heat by flicking their tails in the air. Ask yourself:

How can a simple tail equip them for either extreme heat or extreme cold? This animal is some sort of freak of nature.

DEFENSE MECHANISMS

Black squirrels are equipped with short toenails or claws that are kept razor sharp by all the climbing and scuttling and burrowing they perform (ugh, just think about those nasty claws sinking into your flesh as they climb up your torso and rip your face off). They also have long, flat teeth that can deliver a seriously nasty bite wound that you can bet will fester. Of course, the squirrels rarely have to employ tooth and claw because they are so quick and clever that they are rarely captured. But don't think for a minute that they don't fantasize about sinking their teeth into you.

SURVIVAL TACTICS

Like all squirrels, the ones of Mirkwood are opportunistic eaters. They'll eat almost anything from insects to baby birds to crumbs from the meal of a fellowship of traveling Dwarves—I wouldn't put it past them to eat the Dwarves themselves. But their primary food sources are nuts and seeds, which they tend to hoard.

Mirkwood squirrels are protective of their food stores in a way that verges upon paranoia. The squirrels gather seeds and nuts and hide their treasures for later consumption. But there is also a great deal of strategy and deception involved. They don't just bury a nut and come back for it in the winter. They bury it, dig it up a short while later, and rebury it somewhere else. They also often dig holes and pretend to bury a seed or nut, all the while hiding the morsel in their cheek. These tactics confound and deter would-be thieves and help insure the safety of their food stores. They probably set some kind of weird squirrel traps in the holes, too—I wouldn't put it past the creepy little bastards.

DWELLINGS

If you look closely at the trees in Mirkwood, you may notice ominous clumps of leaves hanging in the high branches. These nests are common dwellings for the squirrels because they can be constructed quickly. They are typically built in a sturdy part of the tree where several branches diverge from a large limb. Twigs or vines are woven together and padded with leaves, tree bark, and moss.

The Mirkwood squirrels may also live in deep, dark holes in trees—either abandoned bird holes or hollowed-out cavities. These kinds of dens tend to provide better protection from the elements.

Black squirrels typically build a number of different nests. They will roam within a mile radius of their primary nest whilst foraging and like to have additional hideouts where they can seek quick refuge from predators—though I'm not sure what creature would want to stalk a Mirkwood squirrel. Temporary shelters may include holes in the ground, hollow logs, and fallen trees. They often construct alternate exits for quick escapes and conceal these "back doors" with leaves. They usually keep a cache of food stored somewhere near each of their temporary nests.

SQUIRREL WISDOM

If you are inclined to stoop as low as a dark, scuttling forest rodent, you can glean quite a few pearls of wisdom from the Black Squirrels of Mirkwood. The nasty animals are excellent examples of adaptability. By studying and emulating the behavior of these creatures, you can learn some incredibly useful survival skills—provided you have absolutely no standards.

Here are some ways to think like a squirrel that may very well save your sorry, despicable life:

- **Blend in.** Employ some method of camouflage so you are better able to hide or go unnoticed. And then scuttle around in the dark, unseen. Watch your enemies as they go about their business, unaware of your presence. Heck, watch your friends, too. You might as well.

- **Always be prepared.** Stash secret stores of food and supplies in several key locations to allow yourself easy access to what you need when you are on the run or in hiding. Don't bother sharing with the rest of us. You like to hoard stuff, don't you?

- **Be ready to travel light.** Since you're only out for yourself, you'll want to be able to move quickly. Having backup supplies stashed somewhere nearby allows you to leave at a moment's notice and move quickly. Oh, that's just great. Don't let anyone know where you're going or how to get in touch. Just turn your back on everyone and everything.

- **Stay alert.** Awareness is key; pay attention to your environment and surroundings, and be wary of sudden changes that imply danger. You always were a little twitchy.

- **Retreat is always an option.** A quick escape is key to survival; always have a back door. Just get out of here already, you beastly thing.

20 Rings of Gold

A Cautionary Tale of True Obsession

Three rings for Elven kings under the sky;
Seven for Dwarf Lords in their halls of stone;
Nine for mortal men, doomed to die;
One for the dark lord on his dark throne.
In the Land of Mordor where the Shadows lie.
One ring to rule them all, one ring to find them.
One ring to bring them all and in the darkness bind them.
In the land of Mordor where the shadows lie.

—From J.R.R. Tolkien's *The Lord of the Rings*

What is the nature of pure obsession? What happens when desire for something obscures all else and becomes the sole driving force of one's existence? To ponder such a question is to catch a glimpse into the mind of a Ringwraith. Also known as the infamous Nazgûl, the Ringwraiths became servants of evil because of their devotion to rings granted to them by the Dark Lord Sauron.

A Ringwraith's descent into obsession is gradual, and its insatiable need to possess the ring begins simply. At first it may appear as innocent curiosity. Anyone would want to have a look at a ring that endowed its wearer with magic powers. And who wouldn't want to try it out? And owning such a ring, well, it goes without saying that most couldn't resist.

As you can imagine, things progress from there. Wielding power is by all means desirable. And being evil, well, that's all relative, isn't it? What one man might call "evil" another might simply call "ambition." Really, who are we to make those distinctions?

But wearing a ring of power is a dangerous path for anyone, Man or wizard alike. You'll start out using the ring for your own aims— good or bad or whatever in between—but in the end, the ring will make you its servant.

Be your own judge. In order to better understand, let's look at what a diary written by a person going through the various stages of ring obsession might look like. (Disclaimer: The events and char- acters depicted here are not taken from Tolkien's stories. This is a dramatization of the transformation one might undergo as one be- comes a Ringwraith.)

Dear Diary,

Best Day Ever! Today I learned that rings of power were to be distributed among the elite of Middle- earth. It's true. The Necromancer from the Land of Mordor is giving rings to all the kingdoms. Isn't that nice? I guess he isn't really the dark lord ev- eryone's made him out to be. I mean, he seemed all scary at first with his giant All Seeing Eye and his minions of trained fighting Orcs. But it's all for show, you know. "I'm a daaaarrrk Necro- maaaaancerrrrr ... fear and obey me." Sure, it can be a little off-putting, but as it turns out, he's a pretty nice guy, I guess. Who knew?

And to prove his benevolence, he's giving out these awesome rings that do really awesome things like make you turn invisible. The Elves are getting three of the power rings. The Dwarves, seven. And Men, well, we get the most! We get nine! Nine beauti-

ful golden rings that hold such power, one can hardly imagine. And guess who's getting one?

That's right. Yours truly! My very own ring of
power. Can you imagine? Man, oh man, I can't wait
until it gets here.

Xoxo,

Timmy

Timmy sure sounds excited, doesn't he? And who wouldn't be
thrilled to receive such a special gift and such grand recognition
from an individual so powerful? It's like being asked to join an elite
club—very few people would refuse such an offer. Your mind would
immediately become filled with great thoughts and grand intentions.
With your ring, you can be important. You can make a difference
in the world. And then and there you would already begin to lose
yourself—you wouldn't realize it, but your subconscious mind would
already be in the ring's grasp.

Dear Diary,

I can't stop thinking about my ring of power. I
mean, this is a huge deal, right? I've every right
to be excited, don't I? Tonight, in celebration, the
kitchen prepared some of my favorites (there was
mutton slathered with jam and roasted turkey legs
and yams and freshly baked bread and pies and
flagons of ale—I mean, seriously, there was enough
food to keep a family of hobbits happy, for a little
while, anyway) but all I could do was pick at a
small seed-cake because all I could think about
was that precious ring.

*I dreamed about it last night. I dreamed that
the ring was calling my name softly ... like a whisper that could hardly be heard above the wind. It
called and called, and I was hunting for it in the forest. In my dream, I was searching and searching.
The forest was dark, and I stumbled over roots and
fallen trees. Suddenly the moon peeked through
the forest canopy and shined down on a clearing,
and there upon a neatly hewn tree stump it sat—
my ring. I ran and snatched it up and slid it upon
my finger.*

*Can you guess what happened next? I awoke
to find myself barefoot in the garden in my sleep
gown. What a crazy night!*

I sure hope this ring comes soon.

Xoxo,

Timmy

Things are already starting to look a little foreboding for Timmy. A
spell seems to have been cast upon his subconscious. That's how
a ring of power begins to control its user. Under the thrall of your
ring, you'll find yourself exhibiting stranger and stranger behavior. At first you'll wonder what is happening to you, but soon you'll
come to embrace it. Everything that happens will seem like a gift
bestowed upon you by the ring itself.

Dear Diary,

*Guess what arrived today? My ring of power! And
let me tell you, it is awesome. I put it on and immediately I felt stronger and taller. And more im-*

portant—I felt invincible. The ring has a secret I've yet to discover, I'm sure of it. I know not what all this precious ring is capable of, yet I can feel its power surging through me. I feel more alive than I have ever felt—I feel connected with the world, and everything around me vibrates with energy. This ring was meant to be mine! It was destined for me! What great things I'll use it for! Such power. So ... much ... power ...

Tim

Our friend seems to be going through some changes, doesn't he? He seems a bit manic. One might even say he's drunk with power. A ring changes its wearer in this manner—by first making him feel in control and more alive than ever. At this point, the ring may prompt the wearer to perform random acts of violence. You'll become volatile, unpredictable, and intolerant. Not that you'll even notice.

Dear Diary,

You'll never guess who else got one of the rings. My friend Kevin! Well, it wasn't given to him, but it's his now. The original ring bearer, a local aristocrat, was walking through the streets today, making a big show of his new prize. "Ha. See my new ring of power. I'm favored by the Wizard of Mordor!" He laughed and flashed his ring to anyone who'd stop to listen. What a foolish braggart.

He'd gone on like this for a while when Kevin stepped out of an alley and took the ring from him in one deft motion. Really, given the way the man was behaving, he had it coming. Of course, the man demanded it back. You should have seen him. He was so enraged that his face turned purple. He danced from foot to foot as he tried to snatch the ring back from Kevin. The man was truly making an ass of himself, so Kevin clubbed him with cudgel, easy as you like. It was hilarious. And then my friend slipped the ring onto his finger, winked at me, and disappeared around the corner.

I must confess, it's good to know someone else who has received one of these rings. I'm feeling the need to talk to someone about it—I find myself so enthralled by my beautiful ring that I'm curious if the others are experiencing the same thing.

Tim

Tim seems entirely unbothered by the violent act he's just witnessed. He's more interested in talking to his friend to learn more about the rings they possess. And that's how things progress for a ring bearer. As you fall completely under the ring's spell, you'll begin to fully embrace the feeling of power it gives its wearer. You'll feel in love with yourself and with the ring. And you'll find yourself wanting more and more power. You'll never be satisfied.

Dear Diary,

Kevin and I met up at the tavern for a couple of ales. We started wondering about the other rings—after all, the race of Men were given nine of them. Who had them, and what if we formed some sort of alliance? With the successes that Kevin and I have both

enjoyed since receiving our rings, it would stand
to reason that if we combined our efforts we could
accomplish truly incredible feats.

As we talked, a glint from Kevin's ring caught
my eye, and I found myself staring at it. I wondered
what might happen if I had two rings of power—one
for each hand. Would I be doubly powerful? I no-
ticed then that Kevin had been staring at my ring
as well. He looked up and grinned at me. I shud-
dered and drained my mug of ale. Kevin did the
same, and we laughed it off.

Tim

As you can see, Tim wants more. The ring provokes its wearer to
take some action. The wearer feels it's time to go forth and conquer!
You'll start out wanting to use the ring in positive ways—to further
the aims of yourself and your kinsmen. You'll view the ring as an
extension of yourself—a magical weapon that will help you accomplish worthwhile undertakings.

Dear Diary,

Kevin and I are finally getting to try out our rings
for real. There's a skirmish in one of the villages on
the outskirts of the kingdom. The guards were ask-
ing for volunteers to help keep the peace, so Kevin
and I volunteered. I can't wait to hop into the saddle
and wield a sword while feeling the power of this
ring coursing through every fiber of my being—my

instrument of justice. I'll set those villagers straight,
for their own good and for that of the kingdom!
   Tonight we ride!

Timothy

Your successes—and there will be successes—will not satisfy you. They'll leave you wanting more power and more wealth. The part of yourself that desires those things will be increased tenfold. You will become a tyrant.

Dear Diary,

Success! Victory! Oh glorious triumph! We clob-
bered those obnoxious villagers and their silly up-
rising. Who do they think they are? "Lower taxes."
Boo-hoo. "More food." Bring me a fiddle. What a
bunch of whiners and complainers.
   My cudgel set them right. I thumped them good.
The blighters are lucky, too. I didn't run them
through like Kevin did. He cut down some of the
really belligerent ones, easy as can be.
   He's taken to calling himself "Wrath-gar the
Fierce" or something crazy like that. What a card!

Timothy (the Terrible). Ha!

Things will continue this way for a time. Your good fortune will rein-force your belief in and love for the ring. You'll find yourself think-ing of yourself as mighty and invincible. You'll know in your heart that you are entitled to rule everyone and everything. You'll think yourself perfect because your precious ring chose you—your every action validated by the ring itself.

Also, you may begin to notice a sinister inflection and slight hissing when you talk.

> Dear Diary,
>
> The world issss a pearl in the palm of my hand.
> With each passsssing day I gain conviction that I
> am meant for more than ruling thisss paltry village,
> meant for more than the land from the oceanssss
> of the wessssst to the mountains on the horizon.
> My dessssstiny is that of the world.
>
> The leadersss in line before me will fall. Anyone
> who daresss oppose me will eventually kneel before
> me, begging for the mercy of my judgment. The ring
> chosssse me, and I know that in the end itsss power
> will lift me above all othersss, victorioussss.
>
> For now, I must play the part of the dutiful
> ssssservant. I must carry out the ordersss of Lord
> Ssssauron. But I've no doubt that my day will come.
> And when it doessss ... I'll be ready.
>
> T

At this point the ring is your master. And its master is the one true ring created by Sauron to rule over all the ring-bearers. You've become a servant. You'll begin to forget your former life. You'll forget everything but your unrelenting devotion to the piece of gold on your finger.

> Thissss book in my handsss ... wordsss written ...
> my wordsss. A habit, I think ... a curioussssity of
> my passst. Meaninglesssss. I write now, yet cannot remember why. My ring musssst wisssssh that

I do sssssso. Ring desssiresss it ... commandsssss it.
Oh my ssssswwwweeeet ... mine ... my own .... my
precioussssssssssssss...

Understanding the Nazgûl

The Nazgûl are the most powerful agents of the Dark Lord Sauron. They are nine Men who were given rings of power that gradually changed them and turned them into wraiths—invisible to mortals save for their black robes. The Nazgûl seemingly gained immortality from the rings, but at the expense of their free will.

The identities of most of the Nazgûl have slipped into obscurity and are unknown, save for their leader, the Witch-king of Angmar, and his second in command, Khamûl, the black Easterling.

NAMES OF THE NAZGÛL

Throughout Middle-earth, the Nazgûl are known by many different names—all of them sinister and steeped in mystery and legend. The names may change, but they are usually only spoken in hushed voices and whispers. Here are some of the names the Nazgûl have gone by throughout the ages:

- Ringwraiths

- The Shadows

- The Servants of Sauron

- The Nine Servants of the Lord of the Rings

- Úlairi—as known in the Elvish language of Quenya

- Dark Riders or Black Riders—so called when they are seen mounted on a black steed

- Fell Riders or Black Wings—so called when seen riding a fell beast (a flying creature similar to a dragon)

- Shriekers—as referred to at times by Orcs

MOUNTS

The Nazgûl are known to sometimes ride frightening black horses that have been bred in the service of Sauron. While they are not actually demonic, these nightmarish steeds have known nothing but evil in their lives and are trained to serve the Dark Lord. At other times, the Nazgûl ride dragonlike flying creatures known as fell beasts, hell-hawks, or Nazgûl-birds.

WEAPONS

While the Nazgûl sometimes use swords or maces, the chief weapon of the Nazgûl is the Morgul blade, a magical dagger that breaks off in its victim. The shard of the blade works like poison to slowly and painfully transform the poor soul into a wraith himself. The herb athelas (or kingsfoil) may be used to slow the poison, but only Elvish healing methods offer a cure.

OTHER POWERS

The Nazgûl have a dark influence that can overpower anyone in their presence. Simply being in the vicinity of a Ringwraith can cause unconsciousness, terrible nightmares, and even death. This strange power is sometimes known as "the Black Breath."

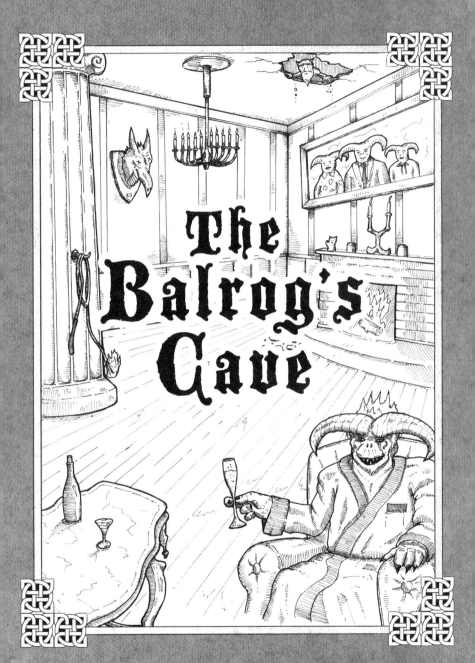

I remember it as if it were yesterday.

Which it was, if you look at it from a certain perspective. If you are like me, time assumes a strange aspect. The individual years no longer seem to matter, and they fuse together into a whole—particularly if you have spent the overwhelming majority of them living underground, with no sun or moon to tell you the time of day, the month, or even the year. I have a sense of time passing, of course. All mortal beings have that. But I cannot tell you how many years have passed since Morgoth told us he had solved the mysteries of the universe and we were going to be just like angels, only on fire most of the time.

Well, just see how that turned out.

I must admit, I had my doubts from the start. Not that I raised those questions openly. One refrained from raising questions around Morgoth, at least if you knew what was good for you. But when the forces of the Valar ran amok through Angband, yelling and screaming like a lot of banshees, I must admit it occurred to me that I'd probably backed the wrong side.

Still, it was too late to do anything about it at that point. Along with the others, I took to the Underdark ways, scurrying along tunnels delved by goodness knows what. Not very easy, I can tell you. Some of my fellow demons (well, that's what we're called these days; not a very nice name, but what do you expect from a bunch of Elvish, degenerate ... never mind, this isn't the time to get into that) got stuck and lay there wiggling their hind quarters, shrieking their heads off, as if that was going to do anything. Several of them actually brought the roof down with their noise, and that just made things worse.

I was one of the lucky ones. I ran and clawed and scraped and fought my way through the tunnels until I was reasonably sure I was clear of the mob. All I wanted to do was find a nice, quiet place to settle down.

And for a bit I thought I'd found it. A big cave, just a few stalactites hanging from the ceiling. (In case you're wondering, stalac*tites* hang *tight* from the ceiling, while stalag*mites* have to use *might* to rise from the floor. That's how I remember the difference.) I shared it with some bats, most of whom, once they'd gotten over the shock of seeing me, were pretty reasonable. Being what I am, I didn't need food, and I was content to sit and relax in meditation. Once a cave troll came meandering down into the cavern, and I had the first snack in several hundred years, but apart from that it was a very calm, peaceful sort of place. Some type of fungus covering many of the rocks made the cavern glow for several hours at a time, illuminating my home in a gentle, warm light. Its ceilings were quite high—several hundred feet at least—and I could sit in the center of it, legs crossed, wings folded (remind me to go on at length later about the uselessness of wings for a creature that lives underground) and center myself for weeks at a time.

My home was an altogether idyllic environment. I still miss it.

And then, of course, that imbecile Morgoth had to go and get himself mixed up with Ungoliant, and we all had to come to his rescue.

Pathetic, really. I mean, here's the leader of the world—in his own mind, maybe—ruler of Middle-earth, tangled up in the web of this gigantic spider, shrieking and carrying on as if his world is about to come to an end. And out of every crook and cranny come streaming Balrogs, intent on rescuing their master from the consequences of his own folly. As I say: Pa-the-tic!

Well, we got him untangled and straightened out, and then he told us his big plan for the conquest of Middle-earth. Of course, there was no room in any of it for questioning, for military analysis, for a bit of plain common sense. Personally, I've never seen what this let's-conquer-Middle-earth-it'll-be-great-and-we'll-all-be-rulers-of-the-world business is all about. I know, I know, Morgoth's been on about it for centuries, but really, when it comes down to it, I'd rather leave well enough alone. If the Elves and Dwarves want this place for themselves, I say let them enjoy it. But I wasn't given a say in the matter. So off to war we went.

Anyone could have told him it was going to be a disaster. For a start, Morgoth always relied on Orcs, and if there's one thing that a millennia of existence has taught me, it's that the word *Orc* means "unreliable." If you want any enterprise to succeed, kill all the Orcs within fifty miles of you before you start. We were each given an army to command, with permission to lop off as many heads as necessary to ensure obedience. Well, if that's the idea of effective motivation, we might as well have slaughtered the whole army before we even got to grips with the enemy. In any case, the whole thing was a complete fiasco.

During the final battle of the war, with everyone being killed left and right, I did the only sensible thing—the only thing that *could* be done—and got out of there. It's never easy for someone of my size to sneak away in the middle of a battle. Fortunately a couple of other Balrogs were in the process of staging a fight-to-the-last-drop-of-blood stand, and all the attention was on them.

I merely slipped behind some rocks, dug a quick hole that went straight down about fifty feet, struck a disused tunnel, and vanished.

(Note: One of the things that strikes anyone who spends anytime living underground in Middle-earth is the enormous number of tunnels there seem to be. Dwarves, with their typical arrogance, tend to assume that they or their ancestors created them and just forgot to tell anyone about them. I think the more sensible explanation is that the world has been inhabited in ages past by older races and beings who made the tunnels for their own purposes, which we cannot fathom. But who listens to me?)

I spent quite a long time journeying, since I wanted to put as much distance between me and the disaster as possible. I know everyone thinks Balrogs are terribly warlike, but in truth, most of us just want to be left alone. That was my thought: *Where can I go where I'm not likely to be disturbed?*

You may be wondering how I saw anything, since there was no light. The answer is two-fold. First, Balrogs, like most creatures that live underground, can see reasonably well in the dark. Not as well as some, but well enough that I rarely banged my head on a low roof or stubbed my toe on a rough patch of the floor. The other answer is that if things got too bad, I could turn on my fire, the sight of which was visible for several miles.

For the most part, I was undisturbed in my wanderings. After several weeks, I ran into a party of Orcs—goodness knows what they were doing that deep in the earth. They had probably wandered into the entrance of one of the tunnels and were trying to find their way back to shallower levels. I was startled but glad of the company. Sadly, they were startled as well and couldn't forgo putting a couple of arrows into me and hacking at me with their swords.

Most Orcs are cowardly in addition to being incompetent, but it wasn't the case with this bunch. I swatted a few of them away and tossed one of them into a handy hole from which I could hear his screams for a good half minute or so before he hit the bottom. The rest drew back, consulted each other, and rushed me.

You'd think they'd have thought twice about this. I drew my sword, which burst into flame, but they didn't slow even then. I took one good swing and the first five of them collapsed, sans heads.

That gave the rest of them pause, and they retreated again. I could see they wanted to scuttle away, so I said, as calmly and quietly as possible, "Look, we're all on the same side here, more or less. Let's sit down and chat a bit. Perhaps we can come to some arrangement."

Evidently this didn't come out as quietly and reasonably as I'd intended, and one or two of them shrieked and shot more arrows at me. I should note that although I can be hurt by some swords—mostly magical ones—arrows have little to no effect on me and are little more than an annoyance. They certainly annoyed me in this case. I gave a great bellow, and half the ceiling fell in on what was left of the Orcs.

It was a pity, because with the lack of company, I was going a little crazy. I resolved that with the next bunch of Orcs or trolls I ran into, I would try to be more conciliatory (although it's hard to be conciliatory when people are shooting arrows at you).

***

After many days of traveling (quite possibly years; as I said before, it's hard to keep track of time underground), I came to a vast open space. I lit up my fires and discovered, somewhat to my surprise, that I was standing on the shores of an underground lake. It was big enough that I couldn't see the far shore. But along the shore where I was standing were boulders and pebbles—some of the rocks almost as large as me. Above all, there was blessed silence. I listened intently and could hear nothing except the occasional splash of a wave on the beach. This intrigued me; with no wind, the water should have been perfectly still. And yet it stirred, evidently by small air currents. Far out in the water, something breached the surface, and I realized there were actually fish jumping, creating ripples and small eddies that ran together.

The ceiling arched over the lake far above me, at least three or four hundred feet. Glorying in the openness of the space and wanting to survey it further, I did something I had been unable to do before in my journey: I spread my wings and lifted into the air.

It was glorious! The light of my flames reflected on the waters and spread across them as I soared overhead. Unable to stop myself, filled with a wild exultation, I swooped and dived, seized by a joy I had not experienced in centuries. Then I concentrated myself and flew forward.

The lake, as much as I could determine, was eight or ten miles across and twice as broad. It had no islands and was surrounded on three sides by steep, rocky cliffs. The tunnel through which I had come was apparently the only means of entrance or egress. That was fine with me. It meant the area was easily defensible, quiet, and unlikely to be discovered. The lake itself seemed to be fed partly by several streams that trickled down the rocks from above and quite possibly by springs hidden below its surface. Once again, fish were jumping, and once or twice the waters stirred in such a way that made me think larger creatures lurked within it. After flying for an hour or two, enjoying the feeling of stretching my wings and the speed and freedom of my flight, I returned to the shore and looked for a place to make my lair.

You may be wondering what a Balrog's lair looks like. My needs are remarkably simple. I don't need to sleep, although I do, on occasion. I eat minimally and can go for several centuries without food. Here the lake's fish seemed to offer a likely supply of food when it became necessary, and since my feeding was so infrequent, there was no danger of my exhausting the supply. I cleared away a space between several large boulders, found a rock with a nook in it that resembled a seat looking out over the subterranean waters, and settled in.

***

During the first two thousand years of my residence, I admit that I succumbed to boredom from time to time. Balrogs were created by Morgoth to be creatures of war, and I sometimes missed the flash of bright steel, the clash of swords, the spurt of newly spilt blood, and the shrieks of the dying. But then I remembered what a disaster the last battle of the War of Wrath had been and was content with my choice of isolation. Fish, as I had foreseen, were easy to catch, but I spent most of my time sitting on my seat overlooking the lake, contemplating my past. I barely gave a thought to the future. Above me, the wars of Men, Elves, and Dwarves might go on, but I cared nothing for them. I was alone with my thoughts and the darkness.

Sometimes, for exercise, I flew over the lake and then perched on crags among the cliffs that lined its shores. I discovered small bats who clung to the cavern ceiling, flying in and out of cracks in the rock that evidently led to higher levels. Looking closely at the cavern ceiling, I found thin veins of silver running through it, forming intricate patterns that I studied and traced for amusement. They glowed silver and red by the light of my fire, so the roof of the cavern seemed to be made of branching lines of flame.

It was sometime during the third millennium that I made my greatest discovery. I had flown many times around the cavern's walls, but curiously I had rarely inspected those parts that lay close to the beach on which I made my home. Now I discovered a large crack in the wall, wide enough for me to pass through. Deeply curious, I squeezed between the rocks and followed a narrow passage that led upward. The ground was rough beneath my feet, and I expected at any moment for the path to end, but it wound steadily up. Finally, after some hours, I realized with a start that I was no longer climbing a slope but was ascending a staircase. The stairs were rough-hewn but certainly made by mortal hand. They circled, and the passage grew wider. Several times, the walls dropped away, and the stairs led across great bridges, surrounded on either side by abysses of unknowable depth. And yet they continued up.

I did not ignite my flames, for I felt, rather than heard, the presence of other beings, and I did not wish to be discovered. Still, I continued climbing, and now the stair grew narrower again. It was impossible for me to tell how high I had climbed. Ahead of me I saw a curious glow, blue-white in color, that made the rocks shine. Eagerly, I pressed forward, rounded the last curve, and stood transfixed at the sight that met me.

Before me, through an arched door, was the open air and the sky. I stepped out of the door and found myself on a narrow ledge of rock. On either side was a vast mountain scape of towering peaks and snowy slopes. In the open air, I burst into flame. Lifting my sword to the sky, I gave a great shout that rumbled and echoed around me. An enormous mass of snow just below the place where I stood rumbled and rushed down the mountainside.

The ledge was, as I have said, narrow. There was no rail or curb, and below me was a great nothingness through which angry birds swooped and called.

I wondered about the staircase and who had built it. It didn't seem to serve any useful purpose. From where I stood, there was no way to descend the mountain—save by jumping. There was nothing to see but mountain upon mountain, although the one I was standing on appeared to have one of the highest peaks. The wind whistled about me; I had almost forgotten what wind felt like.

I spread my wings and rose into the air. All about me stretched the mountains. Far in the distance, I could see that the slopes fell to the floor of a plain, but I had no desire to go in that direction.

The Unofficial Middle-earth Monster's Guide

There lay the world of Men and Elves, and if the past millennia had taught me anything, it was that I was well off without them. I folded my wings and glided back to the ledge.

I remained there for a long time—perhaps a century or more. After the long darkness of the lake cavern, it felt good for a time to see the sun rise and set and to feel the wind on my face. I watched the birds build their nests and raise their young, and I saw the snows melt every spring and return every winter. At last, after a final flight around my mountain aerie, I returned to the stairs and to the long descent back to the lake.

It was comforting, somehow, to know that although I reveled in the darkness and solitude of my existence, whenever I wished I could ascend the Endless Stair from the roots of my mountain to its highest peak.

The damp darkness of my lakeside home was comforting after a long absence, but after a while I found myself growing somewhat restless. Perhaps, I thought, I *should* return to the world, if only to find out what had transpired in my absence. Not that I was optimistic. Morgoth had clearly lost the war, and if I was any judge, that would mark his final defeat. A few of his followers might have survived, like me, by crawling into dark places and hiding, but doubtless they had been rendered helpless. I turned the matter over in my mind for a long time, returning on several instances to the aerie for further contemplation. What decision I might have finally made I don't know; I think I probably would have emerged from my retreat. In any case, the matter was taken suddenly and decisively out of my hands.

***

After five millennia of peace and quiet, I thought at first that I was hearing things.

I was on my way up the Endless Stair and was crossing one of its bridges when I distinctly heard the noise of hammering. I stopped and listened for some time. There was no question that the regular *tap-tap-tap* was made by a hammer, but where was it coming from? I lofted myself on my wings and flew over the deep pit that yawned at one side of the bridge. A spacious gallery lay on the other side, and I alit and listened again. I could hear the hammering coming from some point in the darkness ahead of me. I fancied, from time to time, that I could hear the sound of voices, though I didn't recognize the language. Not like an Orc's, certainly. Even after five thousand years that tongue would have been familiar.

I was both intrigued and cautious. Not frightened, since I could more than handle any conflict unless another Balrog were involved. And I was confident that no other of my race had found his way down to my sanctum. We have a sense when another of our kind is about, and I felt nothing. No, this was something else. I advanced some way forward, listened again, and then advanced farther.

Dwarves! It had to be Dwarves. There is a distinct sound made by a Dwarvish hammer.

Well, that was hardly surprising. Assuming that Dwarves still survived in the world, they tended toward caves, and once in a cave, their first act would be to set up a forge and start mining for precious metals. So sooner or later one would expect them to venture into my little corner of Middle-earth. But was it anything to be concerned about?

Soundlessly, I retreated to my lakeside abode and considered the matter. I couldn't see any real danger—at most, it would pose an inconvenience, if they were to delve upon the Endless Stair. If need be I could easily block up my end and take other steps to discourage them from descending further. It was annoying, since I'd come to enjoy the solitude and the sense of being removed from the troubles of the world, but there was nothing to worry about.

A century passed, and then another century. Apart from being cautious in my ascent of the staircase—a journey I made only twice in those two hundred years—my mode of life remained unchanged.

And then, shockingly, the hammering sounded above the ceiling of the lake itself. This was disturbing. The lake and its grotto lay far, far below the deepest delvings of the Dwarves. Yet now they were penetrating close to it. What was compelling them to dig this deep? I flew again and again along the ceiling of the grotto, my flames reflected in the veins of silver. Louder and louder over the next years came the sounds of Dwarvish shovels and hammers.

My anger was growing. I had been here from time immemorial. I had disturbed no one, had harmed no one. I could rightfully claim this underground kingdom as my own by right of occupation. I alone valued its beauty, its peace, its silence. Who were these Dwarves to pollute it with their presence? As I listened to the knocking of their tools, wrath flamed within me, and my fire burned bright. I drew my sword and looked at it. It had been a long time—a thousand years or more—since I had held the blade in my hand. Yet the time was drawing near, I could see, when I would have to use it again.

The knocking and pounding was coming very close now. Surely there could be no more than five or ten feet separating the very bottom of the Dwarvish pit from the roof of my home. I had to act *now* to prevent further damage. Their trespass could no longer be tolerated.

I waded out in the waters of the lake, something I had not done before. My fire was quenched, but now I was a thing of slime, nursing strength beyond anything of this world. Deeper the waters closed above my head. I half walked, half swam to the middle of the lake, directly below that part of the ceiling threatened by the Dwarves. I unfolded my wings, drew my sword, and gave a mighty push. I flew upward, breaking the surface of the water in a huge wave. As I shot up through the air, my flames burst about me, and my sword glittered and flared. I crashed into the ceiling with a blow that shivered the cavern. Cracks shot across the stone, and great chunks of it fell with a crash into the lake. Below, I caught sight of my rocky seat smashed by the collapsing ceiling.

My fire spread about me, and I became aware of shrieks and groans from small figures seeking to escape the ruin. I landed with a resounding boom on a still-standing shelf of rock that quivered but held.

Before me I could see the excavation of the Dwarves. Tunnels ran this way and that off a central pit, which stretched above my head. Torches illuminated its sides, and carts and barrows full of ore were strewn at its bottom, abandoned by the workers.

Ore. The silver in the ceiling. Now I understood what the Dwarves had come for.

I soared upward, slashing at the thin threads of rope that crisscrossed the pit. At the top of the excavation, I landed once again on its lip and looked about.

A crowd of Dwarves frantically ran toward a great arched doorway that led upward. I raced toward them, sword above my head, and fell on them with a crash. I slashed and stabbed, ignoring their feeble weapons. Within a few minutes, none within that hall were alive.

Kicking aside their corpses, I stepped through the doorway. A broad stairway led upward, and ahead of me I could hear horns blowing and gongs ringing to sound the alarm of my coming. A loud voice could be distinguished, shouting for Dwarvish warriors to stand their ground and defend their Lord of Moria.

The stairway ended in another door. I pushed on it, and the bars of iron on the other side, set to hold it, gave way. I stepped into a wide space, upheld with pillars reaching to a vaulted roof. Arrayed before me was a line of Dwarves, shields linked side by side, axes at the ready. I laughed. Did they really think they could withstand my anger?

A few arrows flew in my direction, and some fool hurled a weighted net at me. I picked it up and stared at it, an idea forming. Even as the line of my enemy advanced toward me, I breathed a half-forgotten spell. The ropes of the net twisted and reformed and burst into flames.

I held a whip of knotted thongs in one hand and my sword in the other. I stepped forward to meet the foe.

A mighty crash shook the hall. I swung the whip and hurled back Dwarves and struck with my sword. They gave way, standing for a moment and then turning. One alone, larger and bolder than the rest, advanced toward me.

"Go back!" he shouted. "You cannot pass! This is the kingdom of the Dwarves! You cannot pass!"

I studied him for a moment. It had been so long since I had fought in a battle that I was surprised by his courage and, be it said, stupidity. He should have known that futile gestures such as this rarely encourage troops—they simply encourage soldiers to run away faster.

He lifted his axe. I cracked the whip, and its thongs tore the weapon from his grasp. With a stroke of my sword I sent his head rolling in the dust.

The others shrieked and ran mewling into the darkness.

***

I spent the next year investigating my new kingdom. The Dwarves had done a great deal. There is nothing like a Dwarf if you want to excavate a city out of solid rock. Some of it I destroyed, assuaging my anger, but some I left standing. What few Dwarves remained I hunted out from where they hid and slaughtered them. Their screams made a palliative for my lost home.

I did not care for the upper workings. They were too close to the surface, too accessible should the Dwarves be mad enough to send a party to retake the place, and I didn't want to deal with the annoyance. Instead, I retreated down into the depths of the mine. My lake was lost, covered in many feet of stone, and I did not have the heart to try to excavate it. Nonetheless, I settled into a place near where the ceiling of the grotto had once been.

Now I wait. It cannot be long before other Dwarves will be lulled by my silence and will dare to enter the mine. They will think it empty, and they will begin to explore. They will sidle along its disused galleries, its dust-choked halls and shafts, and its cobweb-infested chambers. They will imagine themselves alone, and they will again begin to probe into those dark places of the world that should forever be left alone.

And I will be waiting for them.

I will be here.

The Games
Stone-Giants
Play

Vandalism. Destruction. Good Clean Fun.

*T*he lightning splinters on the peaks, and rocks shiver, and great crashes split the air and go rolling and tumbling into every cave and hollow; and darkness is filled with overwhelming noise and sudden light. Bilbo had never seen or imagined anything of the kind. ...When he peeped out in the lightning-flashes, he saw that across the valley the stone-giants were out, and were hurling rocks at one another for a game, and catching them, and tossing them down into the darkness where they smashed among the trees far below, or splintered into little bits with a bang. Then came a wind and a rain. ... Soon they were getting drenched and their ponies were standing with their heads down and their tails between their legs, and some of them were whinnying with fright. They could hear the giants guffawing and shouting all over the mountainsides.

—From J.R.R. Tolkien's *The Hobbit*

Stone-giants are massive creatures made of stone that seem roughly hewn straight from the cliff face of a mountain. These giants are childish brutes with terrible tempers. They love to play games and get into fights with other stone-giants. Often you can't tell the difference between a game and a fight. Both are rough, violent affairs that usually involve flinging massive boulders in some manner or another, and most games result in rock slides or avalanches.

While quite dangerous, the games of the stone-giants are spectacular to watch—kind of like witnessing a really terrific thunderstorm. The rules of their games can be a little tough to follow and understand, since much of the time you'll simply be reeling from the crashing sounds of colliding rocks pealing through the mountains and shaking from the earthquakes created by their sport. But rest assured, these games do indeed (as all games do) have rules—even though the stone-giants tend to bend or break them most of the time (as almost everyone does).

What follows is a general description of the rules of play for many stone-giant games to enhance your enjoyment as a spectator. Your safety, however, is not guaranteed.

BOWLING

Most people are familiar with one version or another of this sport in which the object is to roll a ball down a straightaway and knock over as many pins as possible at the end of said straightaway. Stone-giants use boulders as bowling balls, of course, and trees for pins. Because of this, a game of bowling typically occurs in the foothills of a mountain at a forest's edge. The stone-giants methodically work their way along the edge of the forest, knocking down clusters of trees at a time.

This game is a favorite pasttime for stone-giants, so let's take an in-depth look at the rules they play by.

Scoring

The giants select a pair of tree groves and have two tries to knock them down—this is known as a frame. They keep a running tally of the number of trees they knock down during a game, which officially consists of ten frames, just like a traditional bowling game of Men. Games rarely last the full ten frames, however, before the stone-giants resort to knocking down the biggest tree they can find and seeking out moving targets (such as wildlife or fellowships of travelers) or attempting to bowl one another over. If they succeed at their attempts, they typically count these accomplishments as extra points rather than going to the trouble of keeping track of strikes (when all pins are knocked down in one try) and spares (when all pins are knocked down in two tries), as one would do in a traditional game of bowling. In the end, the winner is determined pretty simply despite the rather miserable attempts at keeping score: Basically, the giant who bowls over the most stuff wins.

Techniques

Stone-giants employ different styles for rolling their "bowling balls," which many of them jokingly call bowl-ders:

- The first method is to roll the ball straight toward the middle of the intended target (whether it be a copse of trees or the legs of a hapless elk).

- The second method is to hook or curve the ball by putting a spin on it as it is released. Doing so can generate destructive force when the ball meets its intended target (or even an unintended one).

Neither of these methods ensures a consistent roll, as the ball is very irregular (as any rock formed in nature would be). The boulders turned bowling balls tend to roll willy-nilly toward their targets, taking out pretty much anything in their path, including the intended "pins."

Delivery

Despite the odd shapes of the bowl-ders, the stone-giants enjoy the pretense of having detailed control over their rolls. You'll hear them bragging about one of three different approaches or styles, which are known as the stroker, the cranker, and the tweener.

- **The stroker:** Giants who use this delivery tend to square up as they approach the lane and attempt to deliver the ball in a very straight roll (which almost never happens) and take great pride in accuracy and finesse.

- **The cranker:** This technique is all about trying to put as much spin as possible on the ball. The giants do this by cradling the ball in a cupped wrist as they approach the lane and start their swing. They try to execute their release and land their stepping foot at the same time while pulling up on the ball as they let go. This approach creates speed, power, and a spinning motion. The effect is much like cracking a bull whip or popping a wet towel at someone in a locker room.

- **The tweener:** A tweener is a technique somewhere in between the two aforementioned techniques. It is a less powerful technique than the cranker but still manages to generate some spin on the ball.

Stone-giants who use the stroker think themselves wise and sophisticated and look down on those who use the cranker. Those who use the cranker tend to make fun of strokers for their pretentious attempts at precision and their fancy ways.

Tweeners get no respect. Both strokers and crankers make fun of them for their lack of conviction.

Ninepins and Other Variations

Bowling games with a set number of pins are sometimes played when the stone-giants feel like taking the time to actually fashion pins from logs. It doesn't happen often, but sometimes after a long bout of bragging, one giant may challenge another to a "serious" game where they vow to keep meticulous score. They set about to create a "real" lane with "real" pins, and the number of pins they end up with is usually determined by how quickly they get tired of collecting logs and carving them into pins. Hence the game may end up being one of ninepins or even five.

BOWLS

In this game, stone-giants each roll larger boulders called "bowls" across a lawn or green toward a smaller boulder called a "jack." The object is to roll a bowl as close as possible to the jack. The bowl that lands closest to the jack scores a point. The game continues until players reach a specified number of points (twenty-one is typical).

This game may be played between two players or by teams, which is interesting because this decision generally determines whether the game ends with a fight between two stone-giants or an all out multigiant brawl that sounds like it might destroy the entire countryside.

BOXING

Boxing matches happen frequently between stone-giants. Sometimes they are really fighting, but sometimes it's just a friendly game of trying to knock each other upside the head. They don't go to the trouble of keeping score or splitting the boxing match into rounds. They just start punching, and whichever giant is left standing wins. It's pretty obvious who wins a fight, after all, and stone-giants tend to scoff at rules and technicalities when it comes to combat sports.

CABER TOSS

The object of this game is to toss a tree trunk the farthest distance. The toss is made by flipping the caber all the way over so that the top of the tree trunk lands on the ground and the whole thing falls away from the thrower so that what was once the bottom of the caber now points away from them. Tosses are also judged by how straight the caber lays upon landing—the perfect toss lands with the pole pointing directly away from the thrower as if at twelve o' clock.

CRICKET

This game of bats, balls, and wickets never happens in the mountain passes. Never. Stone-giants may talk about the virtues of cricket and sometimes try to get a game started, going so far as to set up wickets made from the stumps of trees, but the rules of cricket are so convoluted and silly that the stone-giants give up rather quickly. Instead, they may opt for a game of rounders or croquet, or they may just go ahead and have a good, old-fashioned, no-holds-barred brawl (usually started over an argument concerning the rules of cricket).

CROQUET

Stone-giants enjoy this traditional game using a mallet made from a tree to knock smaller boulders through a course of hoops fashioned out of bent tree saplings. This is one of the more cordial of the games stone-giant play. They think of croquet as a gentleman's game, and it is often played by stone-giant families. When you hear a very low rumble in the summer sky that never becomes a real storm, it may very well be a friendly game of stone-giant croquet.

DODGEBALL

Teams of stone-giants absolutely love playing dodgeball. A predetermined number of boulders are set between the two teams. They then race to the middle of the "playing field" and begin pelting each other with the "balls." Players who are tagged must sit out until one of their teammates catches a thrown ball—in which case they can bring a player back into the game. The game goes on until only one player from one team is left standing and is declared winner for his team.

Despite being played by enormous giants using gigantic rocks in the vast landscape of a mountain pass prone to earthshaking rock slides, this version of the game is still less violent than versions of dodgeball played on middle-school playgrounds.

FIST BALL

Similar to volleyball, this game is played over a small expanse of trees that the stone-giants use as a net over which they hit a boulder back and forth. The "ball" may be hit with the fist or with the forearms, and the object of the game is to score points by hitting the ball into an unguarded area of the opponents' field, where they are unable to reach it.

Stone-giants love to make a dramatic show of diving for the ball and as a result leave long trenches and culverts in the earth wherever a game is played.

FOOTBALL

Also known as soccer, this game involves kicking a boulder down the field of play and scoring by kicking it into the opposing team's goal. Stone-giant football goals are constructed of two posts made from trees or logs and are protected by a designated team member known as a "goalie." The goalie is the only player on the field allowed to touch the ball with his hands. All other players must maneuver the ball using their feet, knees, or head. It is also the only game in which the stone-giants wear short-shorts.

HANDBALL

Another team sport enjoyed by stone-giants is a version of handball. The teams—each consisting of six players—pass the "ball" down the field of play with the intention of scoring a point by throwing the ball into a "goal" that is protected by one designated member of the other team, known as a "goalkeeper" or "goalie." The goals, which are positioned at opposite ends of the field, are made of two tree trunks that have been driven into the ground. Unlike most versions of team handball, there is no need to dribble the ball when moving it down the field of play—because, alas, the ball is a big honkin' rock, and it does not bounce well. Players simply run with it and throw it to their teammates in attempts to get closer to their goal. The defending team tries to block and intercept.

PUSHBALL

In this game two teams of stone-giants attempt to push the largest boulder they can find toward opposite goals. It sounds simple enough but can in fact be quite a violent game, as there are really no other rules besides trying to push the rock over the other team's goal line. It is a silly game that usually ends with many casualties.

ROUNDERS

Rounders is played by two teams of stone-giants who score points by hitting a boulder with a bat made from a tree and running around a circuit of four bases (usually flat rocks). The teams take turns at offense and defense. The offensive team has a "batter" who tries to hit a ball pitched to them by a "bowler." Batters are allowed to use only one hand for batting and only receive one "good"ball—meaning a pitch that is deemed in a fair zone for hitting. Batters are called out if a member of the other team catches a hit ball, if a fielded ball is carried or thrown to a base before they get there, and if they drop the bat while running.

RUGBY

Rugby is a game where stone-giants try to move a ball (yes, another boulder) down the field of play by running with it or kicking it to a teammate. The ultimate goal is to carry it across the other team's goal line. The defensive team tackles the player who has the ball in order to stop his progression. If a team doesn't score within six tackles, it surrenders the ball, and the opposing team attempts to score.

Rugby is a rough-and-tumble game and a favorite of stone-giants. They brag about the outcomes of rugby matches for days on end.

SHOT PUT

Perhaps the simplest of stone-giant games—but also one of their favorites—is a version of shot put where they fling boulders as far as they possibly can. Unlike with regular shot put—which has a surprising amount of rules for such a seemingly simple sport—form and style aren't huge considerations for stone-giants. Players must stay within a drawn circle and throw their boulder using whatever technique they like. Whoever throws their boulder the furthest wins.

The game tends to devolve when the stone-giants begin to throw one another.

WRESTLING

Stone-giants also often resort to ground fighting. They throw one another around and grapple, often jumping off the side of a cliff to land on one another and try to pin the other to the ground. When watching a stone-giant wrestling match, one might argue that the enormous creatures are actually fighting rather than engaging in sport, but one might argue that point about any of their games, really.

WATCHING FROM THE SIDELINES

The games stone-giants play are enormous events that cause the very earth to shudder. They can be thrilling spectacles, but they also generate destructive forces which can rival thunderstorms and earthquakes in magnitude. Watching these sports is not for the faint of heart. It is very important to remember a few key rules when you set out to enjoy a stone-giant sport.

- **Keep your distance.** The best vantage point is typically on high ground—a distant mountain peak, for example.

- **Mind your terrain.** Your surroundings are very important. Stone-giant games tend to shake the earth, so be careful that you don't end up crushed by falling trees or buried in a rock slide or splattered at the bottom of a cliff.

- **Keep a low profile.** You don't want the stone-giants to learn of your presence, so be careful not to get too excited and start cheering or booing as you might at a sporting event of Men. If the giants see you, you might become part of their game.

- **Bring a hat and sunscreen.** You should never underestimate the ultraviolet rays of the sun and their power to do damage. Nothing can put a damper on a sporting event like a nasty sunburn, and skin cancer is no joke.

- **Pack plenty of tasty snacks and beverages!** It wouldn't be a sporting event without some peanuts, popcorn, and beer, now would it?

Remember these guidelines, and you'll have a great time watching the stone-giants at play in their expansive arenas. Unless, of course, you get squashed by a flying rock. That would be most unfortunate. Have fun!

Secrets of the Spiders

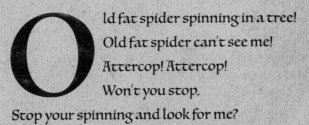

Old fat spider spinning in a tree!
Old fat spider can't see me!
Attercop! Attercop!
Won't you stop,
Stop your spinning and look for me?

—From J.R.R. Tolkien's *The Hobbit*

Are you afraid of spiders, my friend? Well, you should be.

Some areas of Middle-earth, particularly the deep, dark forests of Mirkwood, are infested with giant spiders—creatures feared by Man and Dwarf and Orc alike. Like all species of spiders, these giant arachnids have eight legs and lots and lots of eyes. They are known for their gargantuan, sticky webs and their cruel proficiency for hunting prey.

All of this may sound like quite typical spider behavior, but giant spiders are often misunderstood and underestimated. People tend to think of them as simple, nasty, overgrown insects.

First of all, spiders are not insects; they are arachnids (there are numerous differences, including the number of legs). But more to the point, it is imperative to remember that these giant spiders are descended from Ungoliant, a primordial evil spirit in spider form. Ungoliant is the mother of all the spiders of Middle-earth, including Shelob, a spider who made her home in the tunnels on the edge of Mordor. Shelob was a creature so evil that she lived independent of the influence of the Dark Lord Sauron, and, like her fellow giant-spider brethren, was basically a free agent. The giant spiders of

Middle-earth go where they please, feed on Dwarves, Men, Orcs, trolls, Wargs, or really whomever they like, and bow before no one. They are the creeping darkness of night in arachnid form.

This is one of the secret truths of spiders: They make no allies— not even their own kind. Do not ever assume that you are safe in the presence of a giant spider, no matter where your allegiance lies on the spectrum of good and evil.

EYES IN THE DARK

Have you ever had the feeling that you are being watched? Chances are quite good that a spider was watching you. If you find yourself in a dark forest or a cavern in Middle-earth, it's pretty much a given that a giant spider knows you're there. The tendrils of their webs are woven into their surroundings and alert them to anyone or anything that stumbles into their dwellings. From there you can bet your last farthing they have their eyes on you as you stumble around in the dark. They'll wait patiently for you to make a mistake or wander into one of their numerous traps. And once you are tangled in their webbing, they'll pounce on you and you'll soon be finished.

LEGS FOR DAYS

Despite being giant creatures, the spiders of Middle-earth are able to move quietly, like whispers in the dark cover of night.

Just imagine all the long, spiky, needlelike legs, crawling and crawling, quickly and quietly. It will send shivers down your spine whether you're some high-and-mighty Elf or a mighty Uruk-hai warrior. You'll never hear the spider until she's right upon you. She will attack from above, from the side, from behind or below—but never straight on. The fine, sticky hairs on her legs allow her to cling to any surface—rock walls, tree trunks, and the flesh of her prey. Once she's caught you, breaking free from her grasp is nearly impossible.

A VENOMOUS STING

Most everyday spiders are known for their venomous bites. While bites are certainly scary enough and often very painful, the giant spiders of Middle-earth actually sting rather than bite. They have large stingers that protrude from their abdomens. The stinger of the giant spider injects venom that instantly sends her victims into mystical, trancelike states. While the paralyzing effects are instantaneous, the poison is otherwise slow moving. Spider victims can survive for weeks in this sleeplike state as they await the inevitable.

SAVING SOME FOR LATER

The giant spiders of Middle-earth are renowned for an incredibly grisly method of preserving their food. After paralyzing their prey with venom, they wrap their unconscious victims in webbing and hang them up to later eat them alive. Because of this, many people think that spiders toy with their food, but there is nothing playful in their behavior. Spiders are cold and calculating even when they seem to be leering and laughing. All of their actions have an intended outcome—and that outcome is usually in regard to their dinner.

Spiders slowly drain their paralyzed victims at their leisure, sometimes sampling several different victims over the course of a few days. After all, the poor bastards aren't going anywhere—they are hung in web sacs that resemble a cocoon in the spider's lair like curing meat. In the end, the poor soul is reduced to a dry husk that eventually collapses into dust.

"COME INTO MY PARLOR"

Like other spiders, the giant-spiders of Middle-earth use large webs to catch their unfortunate victims. Spiders employ a few different elaborate architectures when constructing their webs, which are made of protein-based silken threads excreted by the spider. Each type of web serves a particular purpose or enables a specific strategy that the spider uses for catching her prey.

Spiral Orb Web

The most familiar of webs is the spiral orb web. The spider constructs this web by sending out a line of silk that drifts on the wind until it connects with a solid structure (such as a tree or the wall of a cave). The spider then attaches the other end to the surface where she is standing. She then crawls along to the middle of the line and repeats the process a couple more times. Once several main lines are created, she begins to connect these supporting threads with an intricate pattern of radial threads in a spiral that starts at the center and works its way to the outside.

The spider then waits on the edge of the construction for her prey to become entangled in a portion of the web. Once an unfortunate victim wanders into it, the spider runs to the center, stings him, and cocoons him in more of the sticky silk.

Sheet Webs

Sheet webs are what a spider creates when she weaves a close-knit layer of webbing along a low surface (such as a cave floor or along the ground in the forest). This type of webbing is used as an alert system (it is often connected to other webbing by strands that carry warning vibrations) and can also tangle around the feet of an approaching victim in order to slow him down.

Funnel Webs

A funnel web is a tubular construction that the spider hides inside while awaiting passing potential victims. When her prey happens by, the spider rushes forth from the funnel and attacks.

MAKING MORE SPIDERS

If you need further convincing of the unscrupulous nature of Middle-earth's ultimate predators, take a moment to consider how they reproduce.

Females attract males with shrill cries that serve as mating calls. A male spider will gently pluck on a female's web to announce his intentions and then approach the female with an elaborate mating dance, arching his body and vibrating his palpus. This elaborate courting ritual does nothing to endear the male to his potential mate: After mating with the female, males are summarily killed and eaten. Female spiders may choose to mate with numerous males before finally laying their fertilized eggs.

Once the eggs are fertilized, the female spider will create a silken egg sac and guard the eggs until the babies hatch. Once the babes are born, anything can happen. If the mother is hungry, she might devour them straight away and then start the whole process again. If she's feeling proud of her offspring, she might carry them around on her back (all eight hundred or so) until they are big enough to go off on their own. Finally, if they're quick and mean enough, the little bundles of joy might devour their mother before going out into the world and starting their own reigns of terror.

DEFENSE FROM SPIDERS

It makes no difference if you are Man or Orc, good or evil, or somewhere in between; you are nothing more than a potential meal to a giant spider. Your best chance of surviving a spider encounter is to avoid capture. Here are a few ways to protect yourself from these nasty harbingers of death.

Be Mindful of Your Surroundings

The easiest and best method to employ in defense against the giant spiders of Middle-earth is to avoid their dwelling places. In short, if you happen upon a place that looks like it might be home to a giant spider, you should probably steer clear—and it doesn't take a lot of common sense to recognize spidery-looking places.

For starters, you should obviously avoid dark forests. These places are teeming with insect life, which make tasty little snacks for the large arachnids. But the real meals the giant spiders are waiting for are larger prey: stags, bears, Wargs, and groups of wayward travelers.

Also be wary of caves, caverns, and tunnels in the earth. These dark underground places are a favorite home to these mammoth creepy crawlies. Plus, trolls and goblins tend to live underground, and giant spiders have no qualms about having various and assorted monsters for dinner.

Watch for any place that seems to be devoid of light. As mentioned before, giant spiders are supernatural creatures descended from a dark spirit in spider form. In fact, Shelob was said to weave webs made of shadow and vomit darkness.

Aim for the Eyes

If a giant spider pounces on you, keep in mind that the most sensitive parts of the creature are her eyes. If you are quick enough, you may be able to fend her off with a sword, spear, or other long, sharp weapon by stabbing one of her many eyes. The good news is that you have several targets to choose from.

Watch Out for the Stinger

If you are under attack by a giant spider, it is paramount to avoid getting stung. Once stung, you will quickly lose consciousness. If you can lop off the creature's stinger with a sword or axe as she comes for you, you'll be in a much better position—but not safe (read on).

Don't Forget the Mandibles

If the spider is unable to sting you, she can still bite your head clean off with a single chomp from her large mandibles. (How do you think she kills her boyfriends when she's done with them?) So if you are able to avoid the stinger, watch out for her jaws and continue to attack the eyes to drive the creature back into the shadows.

Let There Be Light

A certain nasty hobbit was able to ward off Shelob in the tunnels of Mordor with a magic vial of light from the Elves. If you happen to have a source of light (magic or not), wave it in front of the spider's eyes and she may retreat into the darkness.

A FINAL WARNING

The ways of the giant spiders are mysterious. Their intelligence should not be underestimated. How much they have evolved is not entirely known, but the dark spirit from which they originated was one of the first primordial evils that existed in the ages before the dawn of Middle-earth. One should naturally assume that they are more than what they seem and that they are a pure form of evil that should be feared and respected, if not revered.

Take care when you travel through their dwelling places. Mind your step and tread in the light (unless, of course, you are a troll), lest you meet your end as an unfortunate meal for the very essence of darkness itself.

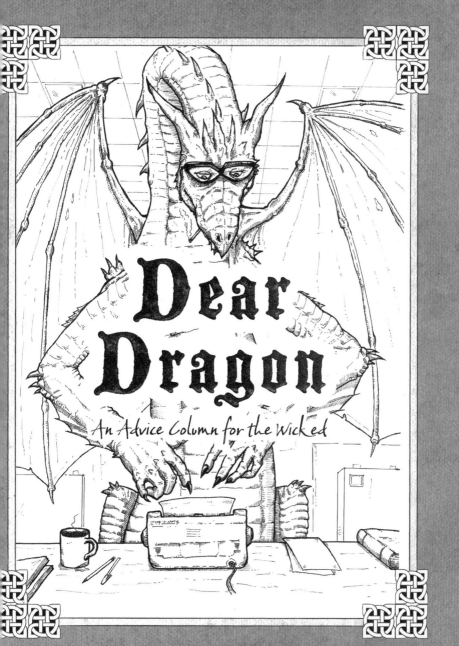

Dear Dragon

An Advice Column for the Wicked

This of course is the way to talk to dragons, if you don't want to reveal your proper name (which is wise), and don't want to infuriate them by a flat refusal (which is also very wise). No dragon can resist the fascination of riddling talk and of wasting time trying to understand it.

—from J.R.R. Tolkien's *The Hobbit*

Dear Resplendent Dragon,
I think my boyfriend is cheating on me. What
should I do?

Sincerely,
Heartbroken

Dear Heartbroken,
Have you tried setting him on fire? I find that nothing brings the truth out of someone like a torrent of flames. Plus, whether he confesses or not—and I'll bet that he will—you won't have to worry about him straying anymore. Charcoal briquettes don't cheat.

Yours truly,
D.

Dear Illustrious Dragon,
Your wings are like satin and your talons gleam
like the finest silver. My neighbor insists on putting
silly yard ornaments out on display. They are seri-
ously tacky. I come home greeted by stone gnomes
and flamingos every single day. I've considered in-
volving the Fellowship of Homeowners, but I don't
want to be that neighbor. How can I convince him
that his sense of style has to go?

Many thanks,
Perplexed

Dear Perplexed,
UGGGGH. Lawn gnomes??? He might as well have a bunch of filthy Dwarves in his yard. I completely sympathize with your dilemma. A person of your impeccable taste—clearly evident from your insight-ful commentary about my wings and talons—should not have to live in such deplorable conditions.

Have you ever seen a village marauded? Well, I think your neigh-bor deserves no less. You should descend on him from a darkened sky, obliterate his front door, and simply raze his tacky residence to the ground.

Personally, I'd salt the earth while you're at it and just start over. The very nubs of grass on his property probably reek of poor taste.

Good luck,
D.

Dear Illustrious Dragon,
The world is in a terrible state, and I think I should
rule it. I'm just not sure where to start. What do you
think? Any advice?

Yours truly,
Future Ruler

Dear Future Ruler,

Oh boy, have I been there. Things can definitely seem like a mess when you're at the bottom of the heap. But you'd be surprised how much better things look when perched atop a mountain of gold. You should get out more. Treat yourself. Pillage a few towns. Raid a few coffers. You'll feel better once you have a treasure you can call your own.

Happy hunting,
D.

Dear Brilliant Dragon,
My husband seems distracted and bored all the
time. I'm afraid the magic is gone from our mar-
riage. How do I get his attention again?

Sincerely,
Lonesome

Dear Lonesome,

Have you ever seen the magnificent scales of a dragon? Scales that dazzle like gems in the moonlight? Have you ever been enveloped in the shadow of expansive wings that block out the sun? A dragon walks into the room and people notice. A dragon demands attention. Girl, you need to embrace your inner dragon!

Say it with me: "I am magnificent! I am resplendent! I am fierce! Hear me roar!"

Now go out there and make your man notice you! And if he doesn't pay you the reverence you deserve—evicerate him.

Good luck,
D.

> Dear Dragon,
> I'm trying to quit smoking. Do you have any advice for giving up Old Toby?
>
> Thanks,
> Smokey

Dear Smokey,
I have absolutely no advice for you. Smoking is a large part of what I do. I'm a freakin' dragon, for goodness sake. We're all about smoke and fire. I pity those who are unable to breathe their own fire and think that taking up the pipe is just a natural part of coping with this inadequacy. Seriously, why would you want to give up one of the premier luxuries of life? I wish I could help you, but it sounds as if you are resolved to continue down this sad path, and I'm afraid you are beyond hope.

Sincerely,
D.

Dear Dragon,
I have a co-worker who pranks me all the time. I've dealt with enough fake customer calls, stolen staplers, plastic-wrapped desks, and motivational posters of cats (cats!) to last me a lifetime. I want vengeance, but I'm having a tough time coming up with the ultimate prank. Any ideas?

Thanks,
April Fool

Dear April Fool,
Here's how you can replicate the best prank I ever pulled:

Box yourself up and have the crate shipped to your place of business. Make sure your "package" is marked to the attention of your co-worker. When he opens the crate, jump out and set him on fire. He'll be completely surprised, and you'll laugh about it for days.

Plus, I guarantee you no one in your office will ever steal your stapler again.

Good Luck,
D.

Dear Dragon,
I received a ring of power from the Dark Lord! Can you imagine? I can't wait to try this thing out! I'm not sure what I should conquer first. Maybe you have some suggestions.

Yours truly,
Timmy

Dear Timmy,

Is that really your name? Wow. Just wow.

A ring of power, hmm? Yeah, I've wondered about those but was always afraid I'd wind up being Sauron's little bitch. Let me know how that works out for you.

Good luck with that,
D.

> Dear Dragon,
> How do I get boys to like me instead of fear me?
>
> Sincerely,
> Mysterious

Dear Mysterious,
I think you just did.

Call me,
D.

> Dear Dragon the Wise,
> I'm worried about planning for retirement. I'm not great at saving money. Over the years I've made several poor investments that have yielded terrible profits—I've had to admit to myself that I'm just not very good with money. What should I do?
>
> Sincerely,
> Down & Out

Dear Down & Out,

You're far too concerned with what you have. You should be more concerned with what others have—and then you should take it from them. Quit sitting around pondering your wealth (or lack of it). Get out there and take what you want. Pretty soon you'll have more money than you know what to do with. Plus, you'll be having so much fun you won't even worry about retiring anymore.

Yours truly,
D.

Dear Venerable Dragon,
My wife wants to have babies, but I'm not so sure.
What should I do?

Sincerely,
Clueless

Dear Clueless,

Your wife is right! You should absolutely have babies. They are delicious! (Particularly with a nice béarnaise sauce).

Enjoy,
D.

Dear Magnificent Dragon,
As far as evildoers go, I consider myself fairly suc-
cessful. I have acquired wealth and power. I have
piles of gold, chests filled with jewels and trinkets,
and peasants who cower before me.

But counting my money just isn't fun anymore. And the look of fear my mandates used to elicit among my people no longer amuses me like it once did.

Whatever shall I do?

Yours truly,
Despondent

Dear Despondent,

You've lost your mojo. It sounds to me like your success has bogged you down and you've forgotten the "art" of being evil.

Don't pillage towns for the riches; do it because you love it! Don't hoard treasure to be rich; the true power in the treasure is in the stealing of it! The money doesn't mean anything. The fact that it was someone else's and you took it from them is what matters. Get out there and scare the crap out of some folks again. Take some candy from some little kids or something.

You'll find yourself back in the game in no time.

Good luck,
D.

Dear Dragon,

I can't control my food intake. I eat and eat and eat and just can't stop. The weird part is that I have very specific cravings. I can't seem to get enough melon. Watermelon, honeydew, cantaloupe ... you name it and I'm all over it. What's the deal? I think I have a strange disorder. What should I do?

Yours truly,
Melon-choly

Dear Melon-choly,

Did you make that name up yourself? I can't decide if it's clever or just plain silly. First of all, eating disorders are no laughing matter. So you might want to dispense with the puns.

Secondly, it sounds like you could be under a spell that some off-his-rocker wizard decided would make for a funny joke. Honestly, this is one of the weirdest things I've ever heard of. It's not very sinister, and no one seems to stand to gain anything from it. Unless maybe the wizard is also a melon farmer.

All said, I suppose there are much worse things you could be craving. I mean watermelon is certainly refreshing. After a long night of breathing fire I often enjoy a slice or two myself—as long as it's seedless.

Good luck,
D.

> Dear Dragon,
> Some guy in our village just got a ring of power and is going around showing it off and bragging about how great it is. He's getting on my nerves. What should I do?
>
> Yours truly,
> Kevin

Dear Kevin,

You're gonna club the guy over his noggin' and take it. It's a whole big thing. Just do it already.

Whatever,
D.

Dear Dragon,

I get the worst dry skin. Do you have any advice for keeping your skin from drying out?

Yours truly,
Ashy

Dear Ashy,

I know what you mean! Do you want to talk about scales? You should see my belly. There's definitely a downside to all the fire breathing that I get to indulge in. But I find that it's best to just go with it, you know? I have scales, so I polish them up so that they shine like diamonds. Perhaps there's something you can do with your own complexion that makes the most of your natural attributes. It's all about doing what you do best.

You might also try wallowing in the rendered fat of some suckling pigs.

Good Luck,
D.

Dear Resplendent Dragon,

My mother-in-law drives me crazy! She nitpicks every single thing I do. Nothing is good enough—my housekeeping, my cooking, the laundry—you name it, she nags me about it. Whatever shall I do?

Yours truly,
Inlaw Trouble

Dear Inlaw Trouble,

Has your mother-in-law ever seen bones burned clean off flesh and then bleached by the sun? Has she ever tasted the fire-broiled meat of a well-roasted pony? And laundry? Seriously?

It sounds to me like your mother-in-law needs a few things put into perspective. She's lording over you because she thinks she's the mightiest. I once knew this dragon who used to stretch his wings every time he saw me, just to show me how big they were. And you know what? His wings *were* bigger than mine. They really were. They were big, magnificent things that shown like fine silk in the moonlight. So I burned them off. Now he's got no wings. Now he just kind of slithers around like a great big snake ... and how scary is that? Well, I guess it's still kind of scary, but I think you get my point.

You need to assert yourself, girlfriend.

Good luck,
D.

> Dear Awesome and Terrible Dragon,
> I just bought a new cart for hauling around my spoils of war. I got it for a good price from this troll buddy of mine. It seemed fine at first, but now the wheel keeps falling off. I can't help but think that maybe the guy knew it had a bad wheel, but on the other hand, he gave me a good deal on it. Did he do me a favor, or did he just pawn his junk off on me? What should I do?
>
> Thank you,
> Conflicted

Dear Conflicted,

I'm sorry to tell you this … but you, my friend, are a sucker. He probably found that cart in shambles on some deserted battlefield somewhere and slapped it back together with a few rusty nails and some twine. And then he sold it to the first dope he could find—you. Do you really think buying anything from a troll is a good idea?

You need to set it—and him—on fire.

Sincerely,
D.

Dear Dragon,

I have some company staying with me who sort of invited themselves. I want to be a good host, but it chafes me that they would just show up and start raiding my pantry. What should I do?

Yours truly,
Inconvenienced

Dear Inconvenienced,

Are you a hobbit, by chance? The only people I know who have this kind of trouble are hobbits, because they're too polite and wishy-washy (except maybe for the Sackville-Bagginses).

Listen, if someone comes into my house and starts helping themselves to stuff, they'll find themselves on the wrong end of a talon. And yes, they will likely be on fire as well.

Take some initiative and throw the Dwarves (they're Dwarves, aren't they?) out on their bums.

Good luck,
D.

Dear Dragon,

There's a girl that I've had a crush on for a very long time, but I'm not sure she knows I exist. How can I get her to notice me?

Yours truly,
Invisible

Dear Invisible,

Are you really invisible or is that just a metaphor? Because if you're using some magic trinket to turn invisible—a ring of power for instance—that might be part of your problem.

If you're speaking metaphorically, then stop it. You sound very indecisive to me, and that's no way to impress a lady. Heck, you like metaphors ... try this one on. Show her your "scales"—dazzle her a bit. Get it? The scales are a metaphor for whatever attributes a wallflower like you has. Unless you're a dragon, in which case I do mean actual scales. Who am I kidding? There's no way someone as indecisive as you is a dragon.

Get on with it, boy.

Sincerely,
D.

Dear Dragon,

My boss treats me like a slave. It's like he's a dark wizard who expects all of us to be under his thrall. Who does he think he is? (Actually, I guess he really is a dark wizard, but that's beside the point.) How

do I make him notice how hard I work and respect
me as an employee?

Yours truly,
Downtrodden

Dear Downtrodden,
It sounds to me like you *are* under his thrall. It's a bad situation to
be in, to be sure. You don't have a lot of options here, really. Have
you tried killing someone he doesn't like and bringing him a severed whatever from them as a trophy? Big baddies usually like that
sort of thing. Either that or they think you're sucking up. In which
case he'll probably lop your head off just for fun.
   Maybe you should just shut your trap and do what he tells you.
Do you hear his voice in your mind?
   Good luck with that.

Sincerely,
D.

Dear Dragon,
I want to get a dog, but my parents don't allow pets
in the house. What would you do?

Sincerely,
Lonely Boy

Dear Lonely Boy,
A dog is a Man's best friend. You know what makes an even better pet than a dog? A Man. Get one of those, and I bet you're parents will change their tune. They're pretty handy to have around

the house—you can have them clean stuff and do chores. It works out pretty well.

If you're still serious about this dog thing, I know a guy who breeds two-headed Wargs. I might be able to get you a good deal. Think about it.

Yours truly,
D.

> Dear Dragon,
> My parents won't let me date a troll. He's big and clumsy and dumb, but he's mine and I love him. What should I do?
>
> Sincerely,
> Star-Crossed

Dear Star-Crossed,
I'm guessing you're not a troll yourself, yet you've found yourself in romantic entanglements with one—ugh, forgive me, I'm just trying to get my head around this one. Well, dear, we can't choose who we fall in love with, can we? And love is patient and love is kind and all that rot ...

But, have you tried *not* being in love with a troll? Isn't there a nice barrow-wight living next door or something?

Yours truly,
D.

> Dear Magnificent Dragon,
> My sister is rather conniving and unscrupulous. She's hoarding the family inheritance. Since the re-

cent demise of our father (slain by Uruk-hai), she's
taken control of our estate and all of our family's
assets. I don't have two pennies to rub together.
And I'm the oldest! Can you believe it? What should
I do?

Yours truly,
Passed Over

Dear Passed Over,
Oh my! Your sister sounds positively lovely! She must be a very
strong and vivacious woman with a lot of spark and sass! Is she
available? I'd love to meet her!

Oh, my goodness. I forgot. This is about you, isn't it? You poor
thing. You should stay out of her way. You're only going to get trampled.

Sincerely,
D.

Dear Dragon,
I'm thinking of dropping out of school. My parents
want me to complete my studies (I'm an alchemy
major). But honestly I think there are easier ways
to get gold than trying to create it from lead. I'm
itching to see the world. What should I do?

Sincerely,
The Scholar

Dear Dragon   213

Dear Scholar,

School isn't so bad. I've metriculated a bit myself, and I must say I've enjoyed higher education. I confess I have a bit of a penchant for musty old books. And there are usually plenty of tender young students around to snack on.

But, you have to follow your own path. Have you actually turned any lead into gold? I may have an internship opportunity for you.

Yours truly,
D.

Dear Fearsome Dragon,
I read your column regularly, and it seems like most of your advice is about setting things on fire. I love your column, and I'm not complaining, but is that really the best way of dealing with everything?

Sincerely,
Devoted Reader

Dear Devoted,
You're about to find out.

D.

Appendix A

How to Apply for Membership in the Forces of Darkness

Welcome. Congratulations on your decision to apply to be a member of the Forces of Darkness. We're pleased you've made this decision to be a part of the future of Middle-earth. The following material is intended to ease your application. Rest assured that though many apply, few are chosen.

Applications to join the Forces of Darkness, Evil, and Lawlessness can be turned in at your local Mordor recruiting station. Most locations are open Monday through Friday from 8 a.m. to 5 p.m. and closed in observance of all local holidays. All applications will be subject to review, and likely candidates will be contacted in person. Do *not* repeatedly inquire at the recruiting office on the status of your application, as this will result in the downgrading of the application and your possible demise if you annoy the staff too much.

All applications *must* be accompanied by the following documentation:

1. A personal résumé, listing your name, contact information, current status as a member of the human, Dwarf, troll, or Orc races (Note: Any applications by Elves will be summarily rejected; it has repeatedly been shown that Elves, although capable of enabling Evil by their inaction, are incapable of actively aiding it. Any Elf applying to join the Forces of Evil will be tracked down and reduced to a floor stain.) The résumé should also include your education (if any); skills (e.g.,

mountain climbing, horseback riding, lock picking, random slaughtering of innocent villagers, etc.); a list of weapons you currently possess and your skill in using them; and a list, in chronological order, of your previous service to dark lords, evil overseers, village tyrants, tax collectors, Morris dancers, or any other ally of Evil.

2. A blood sample for analysis. (Note: If you do not provide this with your application, it may be taken by the staff at the recruiting office, although probably in a larger amount than you would prefer).

3. Three letters of recommendation, written on parchment (human, Dwarf, or Elf skin is also acceptable). At least one letter must have been written within the past six months. These letters should indicate the title of the person or persons recommending you, the nature of their connection to you (e.g., "I worked with Glorg when I was company commander of a band of Orcs in charge of raiding in the Grey Mountains and he was company clerk. I have nothing but good things to say about our time together. He'd be an asset in any position."), and a short summary of your skill sets and what you would bring to the Forces of Evil and Darkness.

4. A nonrefundable application fee of three gold pieces. Please note that if your application is rejected for any reason, you are permitted to apply again after a six-month waiting period, but at that time, a new application fee must be paid.

5. A fully completed copy of the following questionnaire, written in ink (blood is acceptable, but it tends to smear). Failure to answer all the questions will result in instant disqualification.

6. A cover letter enumerating the contents of your application.

ENTRANCE QUESTIONNAIRE FOR APPLICATION TO THE ARMIES OF DARKNESS, DEATH, & DESTRUCTION

Fighting to Conquer Middle-earth for 5,000 Years—Our motto is service!

Part One

Please complete each of the following multiple-choice questions:

1. You are walking through a forest and encounter a nest of baby bunnies. What is your reaction?

    a. "Awww! Bunnies!"

    b. "Awww! Bunnies!" *STOMP!!*

    c. "Mmmm. Bunny stew!"

    d. "Now where did I put that spell that turns baby bunnies into demon-spawn devil bunnies with glowing eyes and giant, pointy teeth?"

2. You are walking along a road and encounter a Dwarf. What do you do?

    a. Raise your hat (if you have one), wish him a good day, and continue on your way.

    b. Wish him a good day, and as soon as he's out of sight, turn and follow him to see if he's up to no good (or anything else).

    c. Follow him and, as soon as possible, plant a knife in his back.

    d. Follow him, seize him, bind him, and torture him until he's a gibbering, drooling mass of torn flesh, and then drag him to the closest Orc outpost for a game of Whack-a-Dwarf.

3. On a journey to a remote ruin in the mountains, you discover an ancient magical ring. Which of the following is your first thought?

a."Magical rings are dangerous. Better leave it alone. Besides, someone else will probably find it soon, and then I won't have to worry about it."

b."Aha! A magical ring. I'll just slip this into my backpack and remember to turn it in at the first opportunity to a dark wizard or some other responsible authority."

c."Wow! A magical ring! I wonder if this is something so important that it will help me to become a Power. Better not let anyone else know about it."

d."Gadzooks! I've heard of these rings. Now I am a Power who can challenge the ruler of Mordor himself! I'll just slip this on for size!"

4. You infiltrate the court of an ancient kingdom and become a trusted counselor to its ruler. What's the first thing you advise him to do?

a. Do a thorough audit of the Treasury Department. That nobleman in charge has been stealing him blind for years.

b. Do an audit of the Treasury Department, the War Department, the Department of the Interior, and the Royal Stables and hang everyone who's been in charge, immediately replacing them with your trusted henchmen.

c. Increase the size of the army, hire every mercenary throughout the kingdom, and start planning the conquest of the king's peaceful neighbors.

d. To hell with planning! Invade neighboring countries and start slaughtering their inhabitants and razing their villages. Now!

5. Faced with imminent death, a true adherent of the Dark Face of Evil concerns himself or herself with:

a. Clean underwear.

b. Clean underwear that's been treated with a slow-acting poison so if anyone else tries to strip it from your body and wear it, they'll die a lingering, painful death.

c. Clean armor. Who cares about underwear? For that matter, who *wears* underwear?

d. Blood-soaked armor and the bodies of my enemies strewn in heaps around me, headless, armless, legless, and just plain *less.*

6. The most fearsome sight in the world is:

a. Halflings.

b. Elves.

c. Elves with bows and arrows.

d. The Dark Lord after catching you running away from Elves with bows and arrows.

7. Define "treachery."

a. A bad thing. Evil should face its opponents fairly in battle, because the Forces of Darkness are predestined to win the war for Middle-earth.

b. Okay when our side uses it. When the other side uses it, it's immoral and wrong.

c. An essential weapon in the fight for control of Middle-earth. However, we should not lose sight of the value of really big armies with lots of swords.

d. I have no time for such nonsense. My only desire is to strike fear into the ranks of my enemies, drive them before me, and listen to the lamentations of the women with a sense of utmost glee.

8. In the event of an unexpected encounter with a Nazgûl, you should:

a. Start running.

b. Salute, bow, and walk backwards until mostly out of sight. Then start running.

c. Bow low to the ground and say something along the lines of, "All hail his worshipful Darkness and Master of Evil, servant of the ever-burning Eye that sees all. How may the lowest of his servants serve you?"

d. Say, "Yo! Angmar! What's happening? Slip me some skin in the name of the Eye!" But stand back when you say it.

9. To effectively command a company of Orcs, you should:

a. Appeal to their sense of loyalty and devotion to the interests of the Dark Tower.

b. Offer them the heads and lower limbs of any prisoners they happen to bring back from battle. Stress the nutritional value of human flesh.

c. Tell them the whips of Sauron will feast on their foul flesh if they don't do as they're told.

d. Pick out the three biggest Orcs from the company. Tell them they have three minutes to kill one another, and if they don't, the entire company will be massacred on the spot. When the contest is over, promote the winner to sub-commander under you, and as soon as his back is turned, slip a knife into it. Tell the rest of them that's the way things roll when you're in charge.

10. When walking through an ancient forest you should:

a. Take note of interesting flora and fauna. You never know when that sort of information is going to come in handy.

b. Don't sleep under any willow trees.

c. With your sword, randomly slice off long-hanging branches, the blossoms of flowers, and the heads of any wildlife that get within striking distance. At night, set large bonfires, chopping down plenty of trees for the purpose. Don't worry about wasting wood. There'll always be more.

d. Find the best spot to start a giant fire that will burn the forest to the ground. You can then revisit the spot and sow the ground with salt so nothing living will ever grow there again.

11. Halflings are:

a. A little people, inhabiting a relatively isolated land west of the Baranduin River. They can change their voices to resemble birdsong, and they smoke large quantities of a mild narcotic called "pipe-weed."

b. An irritating people, probably legendary, who live in holes in sand dunes.

c. A formerly unnoticed but now apparently important little people, four to five feet in height, with thick hair on their feet. They should be carefully watched and, if possible, be captured and taken to the Dark Tower for interrogation.

d. Lunch.

12. What use can be made of trolls?

a. They make very effective doorstops.

b. They're about the only thing on our side that stands a chance of stopping an angry Ent.

c. Because of their size, strength, and stupidity, they can be placed in the front lines of any army. However, since stone trolls turn to stone when exposed to sunlight, great care should be taken *not* to place them in the vanguard.

d. Because their skin is almost impervious to arrows, they can be sent against the gates of a city under siege. Also, since they don't feel pain and don't have the brains to do anything but obey commands, it doesn't much matter if they get killed or not. They're most effective when you set them on fire.

13. What is the greatest threat today to the Forces of Evil?

a. Our tendency toward overweening confidence.

b. Our caution. We'd be much better off just throwing all of our armies against the forces of the West than waiting to conquer them.

c. A small but hitherto unnoticed weakness. The greatest of all powers can be brought down by an unanticipated power.

d. Threat!? There's no threat! We're on the verge of triumph, and anyone who believes differently will be strung up by his toenails.

14. What is our chief weapon in the struggle against the West?
     a. Fear and surprise.
     b. Fear, surprise, and more fear.
     c. The Nazgûl and their power to instill fear and terror throughout the land.
     d. Our absolute ruthlessness and willingness to destroy anything and everything to ensure the triumph of our Master. Plus the Nazgûl.

15. If you could do anything you wanted to, what would it be?
     a. Build a little house down by the banks of the Sea of Nurn and live out my days fishing and watching sunsets.
     b. Spend my days fighting on behalf of the Dark Power in Mordor, slaughtering its enemies, and licking their blood from the blade of my scimitar.
     c. Die gloriously in battle in the service of Mordor, surrounded by the bodies of my enemies, pierced through with a hundred arrows, slashed by dozens of swords, and with the song of battle on my tongue.
     d. Same as c., only with more arrows and swords. And a louder song. And not so much dying.

Part Two

Write a short essay (300–500 words) on **one** of the following topics. You will be judged in part on spelling and grammar, so please take the time to proofread your essay before submitting it.

1. Compare and contrast the ruling and conquering styles of Morgoth and Sauron, using specific examples from history. Describe the effectiveness of each one's rule, quantifying your answer with numbers of innocent victims killed, numbers of cities and towns laid waste, general degree of Misery Index, and other data. Conclude with a statement as to which dark power you would prefer to live under, justifying your conclusion. (Please keep in mind that there is only one right answer to this question. Consequences of an incorrect answer will be ... unpleasant.)

2. Compare and contrast the races of Men, Dwarves, and Elves, explaining which of them presents the greatest threat to the power of the Dark Tower and why. Offer specific reasons, based on their history, cultural attributes, etc. Please keep in mind that general vituperation, while welcome, is not solely a sufficient basis for this essay.

3. Explain in detail which of the following is a superior fighting style for an Orc army: flanking movement, long-range catapult bombardment, siege, encirclement, or blind forward charge while shrieking an Orcan war cry. Assume the army is in possession of common Orc weapons and has no especially superior qualities in its leadership. For extra credit, explain in no more than one sentence how an Orc army conducts an ideal retreat. (Note: Again, there is only one right answer.)

4. What are the Simarils, and what is their importance in the history of the efforts of Morgoth to rule Middle-earth? Why is Morgoth their rightful owner? Cite specific historical incidents in support of your essay. Bring the story as close to the present as possible, justifying Morgoth's coveting of the

simarils. Note that points will be deducted for the misspelling of Elvish names (since one should know one's enemy, down to the strange way they spell perfectly normal words).

5. Explain how the Forces of Evil can successfully conquer the world, destroy all of their enemies, and reign in darkness forever. Be succinct.

Appendix B

A Glossary of Villainy

Angmar: Home of the witch king of the Nazgûl, Angmar is located in the northern regions of the Misty Mountains. It is a cold, frozen land filled with trolls, barrow-wights, and various other creatures of darkness.

Athelas: Also known as kingsfoil, this troublesome herb is sometimes used in a foolish and vain attempt to counteract the poison of a Ringwraith's Morgul blade and stave off the onset of the Black Breath, and as a ridiculous home remedy for a number of commonplace ailments from bug bites to the occasional upset tummy.

Attercop: A derogatory name for a spider, sometimes used by filthy hobbits who have a death wish.

Balrogs: Wise old spirits from the early ages who joined forces with Morgoth and were transformed into awesome, fourteen-foot-tall demonic creatures that shroud themselves in darkness and flame (awesome, right?). Throughout the ages their numbers dwindled, but some still dwell in deep, dark caverns (such as the mines of Moria).

Béarnaise: A delectable sauce made from butter, egg yolks, white wine, and herbs. Delicious on steaks ... among other things. It is to die for.

Black Breath, The: A serious and usually fatal ailment brought on by contact with a Nazgûl. Symptoms of the Black Breath include hallucinatory nightmares, drowsiness, unconsciousness, and eventual death.

Black Riders: The Nazgûl (or Ringwraiths) are often referred to by this name when mounted upon their nightmarish steeds: imposing black horses bred by the Dark Lord Sauron to be as evil as their riders (well, almost).

Bowls: A game sometimes played by stone-giants involving rolling a large boulder (a bowl) toward a smaller boulder (a jack).

Bowling: Stone-giants play a lawn-game-style version of bowling using large boulders as balls and groves of trees as pins. The rules of the sport loosely resemble bowling that people play in actual bowling alleys—only sometimes it turns into a contact sport, which makes it much more fun.

Coney: Another word for a rabbit—which is another word for dinner. Trolls are fond of eating conies. They tend to smother them in thick gravy and wash it all down with barrels of ale.

Crebain: These large, crow-like birds have been used as spies to great effect by many of the dark rulers of Middle-earth. The sinister birds perch in trees, listen to the whispers of travelers, and report their findings back to their masters. Clever, squawking creatures, the Crebain.

Dark Riders: Another slang term used for the Nazgûl in reference to their appearance when mounted on massive black steeds.

Dragon: A magnificent serpentine creature with wings and talons. Dragons are the eagles of the dark side of Middle-earth. They are beautiful and terrible, with scales like diamonds, talons like razor-sharp daggers, and teeth like swords. If you're brave enough to talk to a dragon, try talking in riddles—they just like it.

Dwarves: Dwarves are short, grubby bastards who set up mining operations in once-lovely caverns and caves (and then there goes the neighborhood). Dwarves tend to create beautiful things (like swords, shields, goblets, and armor) from the precious metals they rip from the tunnels that rightfully belong to Orcs and trolls—and those things are fun to steal back when you rip the little buggers limb from limb.

Elves: The Elves of Middle-earth are a bunch of immortal goody-two-shoes. They sing and dance about in the forest, hold the secrets of the West, and generally think they are better than everyone else. All Elves deserve to be drawn and quartered, if you ask me—or turned into Orcs through the use of dark magic.

Ents: Giant tree-like creatures that first appeared in the early ages. Ents are slow-moving and rather boring creatures. Morgoth made a huge improvement on the Ents when he created the trolls (stone is much more durable than wood—any idiot knows that).

Ettenmoors: A wild and untamed region of Middle-earth that is a veritable breeding ground for a whole host of sinister creatures—especially trolls.

Fell Beasts: These large, flying, dragon-like creatures are the favorite flying steed of the Nazgûl. Also called hell-hawks or Nazgûl-birds.

Fell Riders: A slang term used to describe the Nazgûl Ringwraiths when they appear mounted on reptilian flying steeds.

Goblins: A common name for Orcs.

Hobbits: Also known as halflings, these troublesome creatures seem inconsequential until all of a sudden you realize there's an infestation. Next thing you know, a fellowship of them is all up in your business eating and smoking and singing and bumbling their way right into the middle of your plans. They seem easy enough to smite, but you'd be surprised how tough they are to get rid of. They're kind of like roaches. Smiley, happy, sappy roaches with big watery eyes and quivering lips. Ugh.

Huorns: Huorns are semi-sentient trees capable of moving on their own, usually under the supervision of Ents, another set of treelike entities.

Khamûl: One of the nine Ringwraiths of the Nazgûl, second in command to the Witch-king of Angmar.

Kraken: Also known as the Watcher in the Water, this squid-like creature lurks in the lakes near the mines of Moria. Krakens are gigantic and slimy, have numerous tentacles and nasty teeth, and are—in a word—awesome. They make a perfect addition to any pond or moat.

Lembas: A nasty hardtack style of bread created by Elves. Can you really trust a bunch of bakers who live in trees and make crackers all day? Next thing you know they'll be trying to sell it to us with fudge stripes—and it will still taste gross.

Melkor: An ancient spirit of the early ages who became known as Morgoth when he found his true calling: fostering all the evil in Middle-earth.

Mirkwood: A deep, dark forest of Middle-earth that fell under the spell of the Dark Lord Sauron. Mirkwood Forest is a haunted place where even the water has dark magical properties and can lull anyone who drinks it into a deep, forgetful slumber.

Mithril: A precious silvery metal that is incredibly useful despite having been mined by hordes of filthy Dwarves. *Mithril* is very lightweight and extremely durable, which makes it excellent for armor. It is also shiny, so dragons seem to like it.

Morgoth: The first Dark Lord of Middle-earth. Morgoth is Sauron's predecessor (but I wouldn't mention it if I were you; it's a sore subject).

Morgul blade: A magical, poisonous dagger used by the Nazgûl. When someone is stabbed with a Morgul blade, the blade itself disintegrates but leaves a shard in the victim. The shard works its way to the poor bastard's heart and eventually turns him into a wraith who walks in the shadow lands.

Morning Star: A gnarly-looking mace or club with lots of spikes—a very wicked weapon favored by the likes of the Nazgûl.

Nazgûl: Also known as Ringwraiths. These were men who were chosen and bestowed with rings of power from the Dark Lord Sauron. From there, they achieved moderate success as evil middle managers of Middle-earth.

Necromancer: A wizard who practices dark magical arts and is generally awesome.

Ninepins: A stone-giant game similar to bowling.

Old Toby: A variety of pipe-weed developed by filthy hobbits.

Oliphaunts: Enormous, elephant-like creatures used in battle by the armies of the Dark Lord. They have thick, leathery skin that no arrow can pierce, large tusks, tree-trunk-like legs, and massive trunks that are perfect for smiting large groups of soldiers. Seriously, you have to get one of these.

Olog-hai: Fighting trolls who are under a protective spell of the Dark Lord Sauron, which makes them impervious to daylight. The Olog-hai are used as footsoldiers in the armies of Mordor.

Orcs: Sometimes referred to as goblins, Orcs are large, violent creatures that comprise a large portion of the Dark Lord's forces. Orcs were created through dark magic as a mockery of Elves.

Palantiri: These mystical "seeing-stones"—sort of similar to crystal balls—are used to communicate over long distances. They can be troublesome if they fall into the wrong hands.

Pipe-weed: An herb grown by hobbits and smoked for pleasure. There are several different varieties of pipe-weed, including Longbottom Leaf, Old Toby, and Southern Star. All of them rot your brain.

Rangers: A nomadic group of Men who tramp around the forests, consort with Elves, and pretend they have some clandestine, sacred duty to protect their lands from the influence of the Dark Lord. In other words, they are a bunch of silly fools running about in green cloaks.

Ringwraiths: Men driven to obsessive behavior, insanity, and creepy badassery by the Dark Lord Sauron's enchanted rings of power. Also known as the Nazgûl.

Rings of Power: These magical rings—distributed by the Dark Lord Sauron—grant magical powers to those who wear them. They grant strength, immortality, luck in battle, and all manner of mystical benefits. You may or may not want to read the fine print before you put one on.

Simarils: These precious gems of Middle-earth ... Wait a minute. Are you trying to use the glossary of this book to answer one of the essay questions for your Forces of Darkness application? That is just lazy. What are you, a troll or something? Seriously.

Seed-cake: A dense cake of bread with one or more kinds of seeds baked into it. Hobbits, humans, and Dwarves tend to eat crap like this all the time.

Shire, The: The home territory of a bothersome race of halflings known as hobbits. For a long time, this sleepy little settlement was simply ignored, since nothing of consequence ever really happened there. Turns out we should have razed the thing years ago.

Shriekers: Trolls often use this slang term when referring to the Nazgûl.

Sigil: A ceremonial symbol or seal used in magic—also worn on shields and armor as a talisman.

Stone-giants: These creatures are clearly defined by their simple name: They are giants made of living stone. Stone-giants live in the mountains and are fond of playing a number of games, including several different varieties of bowling, shot put, rounders, and dodge-ball. Their games, which typically involve boulders, are played on a massive scale and leave swaths of destruction for miles.

Trolls: Trolls are large, dull creatures. They have plenty of physical strength but aren't very clever. They are typically crude and loud. They care about little and get what they want by smashing things. There are several different varieties of trolls, including hill trolls, mountain trolls, and cave trolls. Their attributes vary according to their respective habitats.

Ugoliant: A primordial evil spirit in spider form. Ugoliant is the mother of all the spiders of Middle-earth—creatures so evil that they exude darkness and live independent of the influence of the Dark Lord Sauron.

Uruk-hai: An advanced breed of Orcs. They are stronger, faster, and smarter than typical Orcs. The Uruk-hai are the super soldiers of Middle-earth villainy.

Wargs: Large dire wolves that prowl the mountains and foothills of Middle-earth. They are sometimes ridden by Orcs. Wargs are intelligent pack animals with a grasp of language and are capable of much more than simple wolf behavior.

White Wizards: Descended from ancient spirits, these guys are trouble. You might be able to sway them to the virtues of aligning with the Dark Lord, but you can't always count on them. They make fantastic allies if you can find one who'll see the light ... um, well, dark.

Wyrm: A slang term for a dragon.

Also Available

The Unofficial Hobbit Handbook
by The Shire Collective

In the age of Men, one must face myriad challenges: epic quests, imminent danger, the evil gaze of Sauron ... okay, so maybe not. But wouldn't life's day-to-day challenges be easier if one were to take a cue from the diminutive hobbit? With *The Unofficial Hobbit Handbook* as your guide, you'll be ready to brave the difficulties, discomforts, and occasional Orcs you may encounter.

- Become acquainted and form fellowships with the peoples of Middle-earth: Elves, Dwarves, wizards, Ents, and more

- Learn about the dangerous creatures that lurk in the lands beyond the Shire: Orcs, wolves, and dragons

- Use hobbit tactics of running away, hiding, and disappearing (with or without the use of magical rings)

So put another log on the fire, cut another slice of seed-cake (is it time for elevenses already?) and curl up with *The Unofficial Hobbit Handbook*. You'd never consider going on a nasty adventure, but it's always best to be prepared, right?